MW01107469

A Thousand
Screenplays

A Thousand Screenplays

The French Imagination
in a Time of
Crisis

Sabine Chalvon-Demersay

Translated by
Teresa Lavender Fagan

The University of Chicago Press
Chicago & London

SABINE CHALVON-DEMERSAY is a French sociologist affiliated with the Centre d'Études des Mouvements Sociaux du CNRS. She is the author of *Concubin, concubinage* and *Le Triangle du XIVe,* and coauthor, with Dominique Pasquier, of *De l'écrit à l'écran* and *Drôles de stars.*

The University of Chicago Press, Chicago 60637
The University of Chicago Press, Ltd., London
© 1999 by The University of Chicago
All rights reserved. Published 1999
08 07 06 05 04 03 02 01 00 99   1 2 3 4 5

ISBN: 0-226-10068-5 (cloth)
ISBN: 0-226-10069-3 (paper)

This book was originally published as *Mille scénarios: Une enquête sur l'imagination en temps de crise,* © Éditions Métailié, Paris, 1994.

Library of Congress Cataloging-in-Publication Data

Chalvon-Demersay, Sabine.
   [Mille scénarios. English]
   A thousand screenplays : the French imagination in a time of crisis / Sabine Chalvon-Demersay ; translated by Teresa Lavender Fagan
      p.   cm.
   Includes bibliographical references and index.
   ISBN 0-226-10068-5 — ISBN 0-226-10069-3 (pbk.)
   1. Television authorship. 2. Television programs—France—Plots, themes, etc. 3. Television broadcasting—Social aspects—France. I. Title.
PN1992.7.C4813   1999
791.45'75'0944—dc21   98-37985
                                                                            CIP

♾ The paper used in this publication meets the minimum requirements of the American National Standard for Information Sciences—Permanence of Paper for Printed Library Materials, ANSI Z39.48-1992.

Contents

Acknowledgments

I wish first to thank the authors of these thousand screenplay proposals. Their work and imagination are the focus of my book.

The present research was made possible thanks to the Services des études at France Télévision, and above all Alain Le Diberder who initiated the project.

I give my warmest thanks to Howard Becker for his continued interest in this work and for the advice he provided concerning the English version. I also thank Teresa Fagan for her very careful translation, as well as Eric Francoeur for his clarifications on the English text.

I am also extremely grateful to Luc Boltanski for his support of my research and its publication. His contributions, suggestions, and advice have been invaluable.

I convey my heartfelt appreciation to Raymonde Moulin, in whose laboratory and under whose kind influence I began all the work I have done on the media, which, without her support, could not have been successfully accomplished.

There were many people who read a first draft of the original manuscript and who, through their suggestions and encouragement, helped me achieve its final form, in particular Elisabeth Claverie, Alain Cottereau, Daniel Dayan, François Dubet, Jean Claude Kaufmann, Michel Souchon, Dominique Mehl, and Isabelle Thireau.

The screenplays were discovered with the help of Dominique Jacquin. During our examination of the material our discussions, as well as our strong friendship, were richly fulfilling.

The many conversations and debates I had with Paul-André

Rosental concerning the screenplays and their meaning were some of the best moments of my professional life.

Finally, I want to thank Dominique Pasquier for the work we accomplished together, for our bonds of friendship that have enabled us for so many years to share a wonderful professional and social life together.

And I dedicate this book to the one alongside whom I read these scripts, and to the world that he has carried off with him.

What if the current crisis were in fact a cultural, at least as much as an economic one, a crisis involving our ability to represent the world in which we live? What if its root cause were our inability to conceive of our society as a source of positive values? And what if the media were both the source and the vehicle of that representation?

These are the questions that will be addressed in this essay, not in a general way, but starting from original material made up of a collection of a thousand fictional screenplays sent by amateur authors to France Télévision.

It all began in the autumn of 1991. Public television, anxious to replenish its pool of fiction writers, decided to organize a call for screenplays. The short-term objective was "to offer a springboard for a new wave of creators, by producing in the near future one hundred first works of young authors, 'idea people,' or directors from France, Europe, or southern countries." The first phase consisted of developing twelve works of fiction either fifty-two or ninety minutes long, preferably bringing together an author just starting out in television and a director.

The call for submissions elicited an overwhelming response: 1,120 synopses were sent in. The success of the undertaking caught even the station managers off guard: every day from Paris, from the provinces, and from abroad hundreds of documents arrived in the mail, quickly stacked against the office walls, and then having to be distributed to a great many readers hastily commissioned to deal with this unexpected situation.

The first phase of the work presented here was carried out in collaboration with Dominique Pasquier and Dominique Jacquin. We were not concerned with undertaking a critical reading of the sketches (a task that fell to the selection committee), but with analyzing them from a sociological perspective. From that perspective all of the synopses were of interest, the most amateurish as well as the most professional. There was a huge amount of material: a thousand synopses, more than twenty thousand pages, thousands of plots, tens of thousands of characters—and yet beyond such variety they all had something in common. Without really being able initially to identify what gave rise to this disturbing feeling of homogeneity in the texts, we undertook to examine them in a systematic way.

It was a very unusual collection of material, first because they were not completed texts, but merely sketches, proposals for screenplays (each proposal included a synopsis and two scenes of dialogue). In addition, the proposals came in a great variety of forms: some were elegantly presented on glossy paper, embellished with graphics and drawings, whereas others were simply loose pages smudged with carbon; they were also of varying size (proposals were generally around fifteen pages long, but some authors had included the complete screenplay while others settled for a brief summary). Finally, there was a range in the level of the language used and the degree of mastery of the rules of screenwriting. The writing in some texts was very sophisticated, in others, quite rudimentary, and in still others, barely coherent.

Yet, looking at all the texts, in spite of their differences, we continually found the same elements echoing back and forth: the same characters involved in the same plots, confronted with the same type of difficulties, acting according to the same principles, employing the same sort of reasoning. This doesn't mean that all the texts were the same: on the contrary, each represented the universe of its author and bore the mark of his or her personal style and unique personality. But they all revealed similar elements, like so many fragments of a common culture.

As a result, all of the screenplays could be reduced to a few rather simple common occurrences: typical stories, a limited number of characters, and a certain number of features that resonated from one text to another, such as settings, events, kinds of relationships, types of feelings, parts of replies, types of denouement, and the way the author might intervene with his or her opinion in midtext.

There was more: not only did we constantly find the same occurrences in very different kinds of texts, which was already in itself a completely unexpected result, but in addition these diverse representations were coherent among themselves. Set side by side, they depicted the contours of the same universe. Clearly these authors had constructed a common world.

However, the scriptwriters did not all come from the same place in the social sphere. The announcement for the competition had been broadcast widely, and the people who had responded presented a rather heterogeneous profile. The data included in their files was most useful in identifying them (the details of this information are provided in appendix 2): there were a majority of men (71 percent), mostly young (six in ten were under thirty-five), living for the most part in Paris or in the surrounding area (in the areas north and east of the capital), covering a very wide spectrum of occupations (from the realm of irregular work to that of the professions, architects, engineers, lawyers; there were also film directors, audiovisual technicians, journalists, advertising people, actors, theater directors, writers). However, they all had something in common: their desire to write television scripts. If they were considered not from the angle of their actual professions, but of their previous experience in the writing or audiovisual realms, they could be characterized as a nebula of people drawn to these occupations and close to the milieu of media production, to which was added a minority composed of so-called outsiders. Yet there was perfect continuity in the subjects chosen and a certain form of agreement concerning the principles that ordered them. The authors' professional experience or their level of training brought differences in the quality of treatment but had no bearing on the nature of the contents.

What was surprising was that the same elements were found in comedies as well as in more dramatic screenplays. Those elements were therefore independent of the tone used to develop them. They were found in the most highly developed manuscripts as well as in the least-polished texts: they were thus independent of the author's degree of professionalism. Moreover, the texts that the jury had selected to be brought to the small screen were perfectly representative of the entire corpus. They were simply the most polished of all.

However, this imaginary television world had nothing of the atmosphere of American soaps or sitcoms. Nor did it deal with universal themes: certain subjects traditionally found in fiction did not appear in the texts. For example, there were no stories of revenge, no stories of destiny (except in the works of historical fiction), and no problems of conscience (the typical scenario of a character faced with a moral alternative, hesitating as to which path to take); the rhetoric of passionate love was curiously absent. Nor was it a vague imaginary world; on the contrary, the themes were extremely specific.

But what was most surprising was to notice that most of the big-screen movies that came out that year were essentially very similar. Everything in those films was familiar. In such and such an image, in such and such a shot, in such and such a reply, we found entire chunks that we had seen before. The fact of having seen the same character, the same expression, the same situation go by five, ten, twenty times enabled us to pick them out instantaneously. And that inspired a completely new reading of the collection. What the corpus had provided was the possibility of reconstructing the network of microscopic relationships that connected the texts, by bringing to light ties that would not have been perceptible in isolated works. The texts in toto had provided the keys for new understanding reaching realms that extended far beyond the limits of the material.

In order to understand the corpus we had to start with a

look at its defining features. Indeed, it had a certain number of specific characteristics: first, it was a collection intended for television, that is to say, the authors had not sought, as do most cultural producers, to address an elite minority, but had attempted to reach the largest possible audience. Next, it offered an unusual perspective insofar as it came from people who would not ordinarily speak out in the public arena: the writers were not journalists, or politicians, or filmmakers, or experts, or even professional authors for the most part. The collection also had a spontaneity about it, since those who responded were free to choose their subjects, and, even though they might have to some degree been influenced by the expectations of the competition's organizers, they had at least not responded to a specific request. We were thus able to see the projects in their raw form, whereas all the programs one watches on television have already been filtered by station managers and modified by all the interventions of the professionals who have collaborated on their production. Finally, it was a sizable corpus, and it is rare to have the opportunity to work on such a large amount of material. Perhaps most important, however, was that all the texts were works of fiction.

Unlike journalism, fiction lies firmly rooted in the realm of the imagination, which means that it does not need to provide an accurate representation of reality. It must, however, meet a different requirement, its *internal requirement,* which is to arouse the interest of the author's contemporaries. Thus in a certain way fiction short-circuits the complicated issue of representing reality, delving instead directly into the rich, profound realm of meaning and emotions.

To do this the author uses characters, objects, contexts, and plots made available to him by the surrounding culture and by available literary conventions. He draws the references that please him and which are accessible to him from a common repertoire, combines those references and organizes them to create his own individual text. At this stage he has every freedom: he uses old procedures, new contexts, classic characters, and more common images; he borrows from his personal experience and from the mass media; he can practice inversions, exaggerations, and euphemisms. His objective is the same each time: to arouse the interest of his contemporaries. The author therefore attempts to *dramatize* these conventions and to *set the stage around a crisis.*

The object of the present work is therefore to *identify the type of crisis depicted throughout this collection of texts.* To do this I have attempted to place all the projects one beside the other and to organize them around a single plot, in order to come up with something that could be said to resemble a "screenplay of the screenplays." I wanted to make the texts speak to each other, to glean something from all of them, in order to understand what they had to say to us. This solution, which resembled the literary form of the synopses, enabled me to account for the feeling of homogeneity that emanated from the material.[1] It involved a twofold decision: first, not to begin by wondering who had written the texts and for what reasons, that is, not to seek from the outset to explain the corpus by its authors. Furthermore, not to seek to interpret the corpus as something it was not: a mirror in which reality would simply be reflected. The approach required from the beginning was to treat the corpus as autonomous and to consider that an analysis of its contents and an intensive observation of it would gradually enable its nature to be defined. Which, in fact, meant adopting an attitude very close to that which the texts themselves presupposed: a spectator's point of view.

1. Paul Ricoeur, *Temps et récit,* vol. 1 (Paris, 1983), translated by Kathleen McLaughlin and David Pellauer as *Time and Narrative* (Chicago, 1984).

One

Overview of the Synopses

What are the historical, geographical, and sociological contexts of all these stories? Some counting was done in order to describe the universe of the synopses in a more precise manner than a purely literary description would allow. The tallying was done for 817 texts, as a certain number of manuscripts had to be withdrawn from the collection, either because authors had submitted a documentary project, a proposal for a series, or for a short film—projects that fell beyond the scope of the competition—or because the text was not available at the time of our analysis, as it was still out with a reader.

But before presenting an overview of the projects, I must say a few words about the form of the texts themselves.[1] Reading a screenplay requires some experience. Such stories can be rather baffling for a reader who is used to finding a stylistic effect, a metaphor, an unusual turn of phrase, to making a lucky discovery in a work of literature. Authors of screenplays cannot indulge in these types of effects. This is, moreover, what makes their undertaking so difficult: they must be able to evoke emotions and create atmospheres without resorting to the usual resources of fictional writing. Their texts are merely the first stage of a long process, the final product of which is not a novel, but a film. In fact, they deliver *written instructions* and conform more to the literary genre of owner's manuals than to that of

---

1. In the excerpts from the screenplays, my own summaries are distinguished by sans serif type.

fictional tales: their aim is not to open their reader's mind to the evocative realm of free associations; on the contrary, they attempt as best they can to harness that realm so as to limit the number of possible interpretations of their work. These authors therefore rely upon very simple and rather stereotypical figures, suggesting casting possibilities so that the reader will immediately associate known actors with the characters in the script. This form of writing has a great advantage over others when one attempts to penetrate the meaning of its content: indeed, writing conventions are not disguised as they are in a literary text, but are emphasized and therefore become more easily accessible to the reader. But the form is also a little surprising. Therefore one must keep the genre and its constraints in mind in reading these excerpts, and be prepared to give the words time to be filled with images. As for myself, it was while I was living with the texts, reading them, that they began to come to life and were filled with living characters. And it was only then that I began to understand them.

HISTORICAL CONTEXTS

Eighty-seven percent of the synopses situate their plots in the present time, showing a preference for the immediate present, a preference that breaks with the French tradition of historical costume dramas.

The works of historical fiction, much fewer in number, span

Table 1. Time Period of Action

	Number	Percentage
Past	77	9.4
Distant past	17	
19th century	25	
20th century	35	
Present	716	87.6
Future	24	3
Total	817	

a vast chronological horizon that goes from ancient Gaul to the present time, passing through the Middle Ages, the Spanish Inquisition, the Renaissance, the Age of Louis XIV, the Grand Siècle, revolutionary periods. Most of the stories, however, take place in the recent past, around half in the twentieth century, with a clear preference for troubled times, wars (World War II, but also World War I, the Spanish civil war, the Algerian war), the great strikes of the Popular Front, the Liberation, May 1968. That said, the stories that take place during the Occupation do not mention the Resistance and its noble deeds, but usually portray events in the daily lives of the French people that unfolded far from the front lines of the battlefields. The vein of war movies has been depleted.

There are two slightly different trends found within these works of historical fiction, a "scholarly" bent, and a "heroic" one. The first appears to have been inspired by the documentary genre. The authors attempt to recount a little-known episode in history or to offer an original perspective on a less obscure period. In this category we find a number of biographies of famous people (Franz Liszt and Marie d'Agoult, Pierre Loti, Edmond Rostand, Lavoisier, Marat). These texts combine a concern with detail and a desire to present more general frameworks of a historical period through the telling of a specific story. They show great concern with realism and with historical credibility, and this is seen above all in the statements of intent that accompany each synopsis: the authors cite their sources, give bibliographical references, and often mention the name of a consultant connected to the project, or the authors themselves cite their academic qualifications.[2] These projects, which exhibit a cultivated and disinterested use of history, also reveal the influence of the discipline of history on the genre itself.

The second approach is rather different. Here the texts bear

2. The authors often spontaneously noted their level of education, which was not an item of information they were asked to provide on their application forms. In general, they are rather well educated, with degrees in history, teaching certificates, other advanced degrees, or are working on their theses.

less the mark of the historian and are more anecdotal. They portray characters who, without exhibiting the superlative qualities of Hollywood heros, are nevertheless bearers of clearly apparent positive values, and who are confronted with easily identifiable adversaries. They are likable, passionate characters, who are pitted against a collective destiny and who attempt, through love, friendships, or a personal or collective plan, to triumph over a hostile environment. The trajectories of entire lifetimes are sketched, characters climbing and falling: humble souls delivered unto exceptional destinies experience a great rise in their fortunes; fallen rulers go into exile; slaves break free of their chains. The plots combine loyalties and treachery, allegiances and defections within social or political contexts that the authors, using a wide-angle lens, attempt to reconstruct.

In fact, these two sources of inspiration illustrate the notion that there is an important difference between the present time and the times that have preceded it. In *Authority* Richard Sennett reminds us that different historical periods have made different uses of history, and that the more sensitive we are to specific contexts and social determinisms, the less sensitive we are to what is permanent in the human condition.[3] And the less sensitive we are to what is permanent, the less likely we are to look to the past for moral rules or principles of behavior that might illuminate and inspire the present. We are clearly living in a period in which this latter tendency is dominant. Whether they are scholarly or heroic, the works of historical fiction we encountered always elicit a feeling of disconnectedness, some by reminding us that there has never been a golden age, and others by waving around values that are of little concern to us. In any event, the synopses never exhibit a feeling of nostalgia.

The fact that the works of historical fiction are so different from the rest of the texts in their plot settings, the stories they tell, and the values they portray, is of great interest to us in our analysis, in that those texts are a true medium for revealing and

---

3. Richard Sennett, *Authority* (New York, 1980).

highlighting, serving as a contrast to the salient traits of the entire collection of scripts.

Utopias of Anguish

If there are not many references to the past, there are also few references to the future. There is a handful of projects that involve science fiction in the strict sense, but they seem to convey a notion that is the exact opposite of that encountered in works of historical fiction: whereas the past does not illuminate the present, the future on the contrary makes it intelligible. Projecting into the future is a way of revealing the insane logic of the present civilization; this has, moreover, been a standard principle of science fiction ever since the beginning of the century, but it has taken a turn toward pessimism and no longer proposes an admiring anticipation of the advances of scientific progress, as Jules Verne did, but a concerned reflection on its paradoxes and absurd consequences. What is striking all the same here, as compared to the traditional genre, is a shortening of the length of time envisioned for any apocalyptic changes: we encounter very short-term predictions, set *in the near future.* One screenplay that recounts its characters' attempts to survive on a desert planet, where hordes of starving young people scour the cities in search of a last drop of drinkable water, unfolds at the beginning of the twenty-first century; another, in a housing project between 2010 and 2050; and another, on December 31, 1999.

We have little time before us, but also little space around us: the science fiction texts no longer lead us into interstellar voyages in the midst of faraway galaxies as they did in the 1960s; instead, they tell stories of containment in close, cramped, tiny quarters: underground caves where people have to take refuge following nuclear explosions, apartments people can no longer leave because the air outside has become unbreathable, or even—the ultimate paradox—public areas that have become places of confinement (the subway or airport without exits, an elevator that won't open). The imaginary worlds of expansion and conquest have been replaced by those of protection and confinement.

Here are a few samples of the prevailing tone:[4]

Futur ordinaire

Through an opaque veil of exhaust fumes and hanging dust one can just see the outline of a six-flat. Inside an apartment a man is lying on his bed. The hallway outside his apartment is filled with poisonous fumes, and a young woman wearing a thick jumpsuit, her face hidden behind a gas mask, is knocking on all the doors, asking for help. After being refused several times she rings Sam Padoque's bell. He sees her on a surveillance monitor built into the wall. Terrified, she explains to him that her gas mask isn't working and she will suffocate if she isn't rescued immediately.

Two predominant themes run through these futuristic texts: ecological disasters and genetic manipulations. The earth has become a huge garbage can that floats through space. Thanks to the benefits of modern medicine individuals with transplants from different donors find themselves burdened with organs of varying age that do not always function reliably and that force the recipients to seek help in service departments that leave them in a state of mind vaguely reminiscent of the despair of the housewife before her vacuum cleaner is repaired. This is a state of mind that demands cruel decisions: "How, in the middle of a strike, can you justify buying a brand new liver for yourself when you've just bought a test-tube baby?" (*Naissez, nous ferons le reste*) and the need for a certain foresight: "Today, they can clone a new body for you just like that. A double of yourself that you can slip into when you grow old. What you need to become young from head to toe. If you have money, lots of money. Like the TV commercial says: 'Take advantage of your youth! have your exchange body made right away, thanks to a personalized line of credit over thirty, forty, or fifty years. Long-

---

4. A list of the screenplays cited, with translations of titles, is included at the end of the volume—TRANS.

term loans guaranteed by the Sta . . . ta . . . ta . . . tate'" (*L'âme a du bon*).

From a criticism of science, the themes encountered naturally slide into the realm of social criticism. For the consequences of all these scientific and technological changes are the reinforcement of a dependency upon those who possess knowledge, a solidifying of social rifts, and a rise in the tensions of inequality. It is clearly not a good thing to be poor in the world that awaits us. The theme of the lack of money is, moreover, found throughout the synopses, sending characters into an ardent quest for money. However, it is not the desperate desire of the consumer that sends them running. On the contrary, consumer acquisitions seem to be of little interest to characters: rather, they seem detached from material goods, and do not appear to derive any pleasure from their acquisition. Nor do we ever see characters go into a shop to buy something. We no longer at all have the mentality of the sixties, when France, happy to grow rich, delighted in her new abundance of material objects. The characters in the screenplays seem rather to spend their money morosely. And going somewhat ahead in history through science fiction enables us to understand more specifically the reasons for their attitudes. In fact, if characters need so much money, it is not because they are looking for more comfort or luxury, it is because financial security is the only means for surviving in a world where less and less is free. Indeed, the logic of the marketplace is felt in sectors of social life that had previously been spared: one henceforth needs money to breathe, to drink a glass of water, to walk in the woods, to sit in the grass, to have a discussion, to have a girlfriend, etc. All of these types of actions and activities have entered into the sphere of the commercial exchange system from which they had once been exempt. Even the most intimate realms of private life and interpersonal relationships must henceforth follow financial imperatives. This situation obviously explains why main characters, who are forced to spend an increasing amount of money for services they cannot do without, and who are therefore subject to increasingly intolerable pressures, have the discouraging sense that their quality of life is diminishing, whereas the overall level of their income has nonetheless increased. This situation is illustrated to perfection by the difficulties Sam Padoque must endure in his apartment where domotics and robotics reign:

> The front door remains obstinately closed, while the apartment's household computer demands the last unpaid rent. Grumbling and insulting the machine, Sam finally uses his bank card, thereby emptying his account entirely. The door opens. (. . .) The heat becomes increasingly stifling. The girl asks for a soda. Sam refuses to pay the refrigerator/drink dispenser installed in the kitchen and attempts to force it open under the vehement invectives of the machine. This appliance, whose defective software exhibits clearly psychotic tendencies, is finally convinced and opens its door. It immediately shuts on the hand that is about to grab a drink, and demands payment of a fine. (. . .) When they go back into the living room, the television, as if aware of the situation, proposes a new line of household appliances to Sam, who is immediately infuriated. He hits the television, which changes channels and offers him a new antistress remedy. *(Futur ordinaire).*

Although there are few works of classic science fiction, many synopses incorporate elements of the fantastic. Sometimes this consists of a simple narrative process that enables the author to pull himself out of a sticky situation, or to provide a plot with a masterly conclusion: an incestuous thief, trying to escape from his pursuers, finds refuge in his mother's womb; a delinquent disintegrates himself; a camper begins to fly through the air; a gorgeous hitchhiker is abruptly transformed into a Norman cow. The fantastic is not just used as a means; it may also constitute an entirely different genre, and it then returns to the classic themes of that genre: transactions with death (which notably involves a tangling of the themes of art, death, and the irrational); the universe of nightmares, in which the borders between dreams and reality are blurred. But what is most original here is that the action centers around the world of technology: we are in a world where *technical objects have assumed an autonomy.*

Machines, which should be the emblem of technical reality, are on the contrary a pretext for an irruption of the irrational. This idea is conveyed in a large number of synopses that focus on the theme of exchanges between man and machine. First, there are many instances of characters incorporating a technical object inside themselves: thus we meet a young thief who has a mini atomic bomb implanted inside him that will enable him to blow up the world if his life is threatened; residents of a retirement home have dentures that tap out rhythms—a good-for-nothing has equipped them with synthesizer sound chips; a boy has a camera implanted in his eye; a young woman enthralled with computers finds herself with a chip in her ear that enables her to capture the memory of every computer she encounters. Things go wrong when she absorbs a contaminated program that gives her a virus that baffles traditional medicine.

We also find the opposite situation, and a large number of technical objects absorb their users. In a figurative sense, of course, but at first quite literally. A great many individuals rush inside the machines that have invaded our houses, their noses pressed against the glass of the screens, in the midst of electronic circuits and liquid crystals. A video camera imprisons the people it films; a computer confiscates the fanatical player who was spending days and nights at the keyboard; a synthetic woman leads the young boy who has created her into the bowels of the computer. A magical remote control enables one to send troublemakers into the off-the-air channel of an unknown TV station. And look out, fanatics of the *Minitel rose*![5]

Les Déchaînés

As for John, he is being held prisoner in the television set:

> When his wife Lisa returns home, she looks for him all over the apartment and finally finds him on the TV screen. She can't believe her eyes. John asks her to press the "return"

---

5. The *Minitel rose* is the term used to describe pornographic web sites, message boards, and chat rooms on the Minitel, the French precursor/equivalent of the Internet.—TRANS.

button on the remote. She does, and he comes back to her. John explains everything to her. Since she only partly believes him, he brings her along for a ride in a program. She comes back convinced. They then look at the program guide to decide where they will spend their evening. Lisa is rather tempted by a love story on one channel, but John wouldn't miss the soccer game on another channel for anything. This won't be a problem; she will spend a little time in her film, and he in his game.

This is only the beginning of a series of adventures: Lisa will be pursued by the young star of the romance film, which will make her husband, who is stuck in his soccer match, very upset; the television will be broken accidentally; they won't be able to get back to their living room. To escape the bandits who are chasing them they will go through a western on horseback, find themselves on bikes in a bicycle race before landing on a platform in a debate on nonviolence.

With the new generation of computer technology, the scope of reality is altered. Characters can henceforth move around in the midst of a universe inhabited by extremely productive beings, on a voyage from which they have little chance of returning alive, since the world of virtual creatures is ultimately much more interesting than that of ordinary people. And it gradually takes its place.

That said, when we look more closely, we see that the situation is not balanced: heroes are actually weakened by their absorption of electronic components that, in fact, do not enable them to improve their performance for very long. Whereas on the contrary, the technical objects that have become autonomous after swallowing up those who interact with them seem to get along perfectly well in a world without humans.

Human beings' sequestration by machines is a symbolic illustration of a major theme that runs through the entire collection of texts: technology imprisons those who use it. Technology captures people because it captivates them, and then it isolates them and cuts them off from any form of sociability; technology is thus in part responsible for the development of the crisis of social interactions ("Adele constantly wears her Walkman so that passersby will not speak to her"). Computer fanatics isolate themselves from family life to carry out their leisure activities; videocassette fanatics end up living entirely by proxy (*Au risque de s'y perdre*). The case of the answering machine is symptomatic: although the telephone is everywhere in American soap operas, as it enables an absent third party to be introduced and creates expectations and repercussions that feed the dialogues, it is rarely mentioned in the synopses: the answering machine is the dramatic instrument substituted for it. Yet contrary to what one might expect, the answering machine is not represented as a means of maintaining contact when its owner is absent, allowing a caller to leave a message after the beep: its essential function here is to avoid direct communication. You can call when you're sure no one will be there to answer (a man leaves the message that he is breaking up with his girl on her answering machine; an anonymous criminal confesses his crimes on unknown answering machines) or screen calls in order to avoid being disturbed (a young woman refuses to call back a former lover who has resurfaced to sabotage her upcoming wedding). A young engineer-sculptor builds a giant pyramid of answering machines resembling a "compressed" sculpture by César[6] that enables him to intercept the conversations of an entire city. No call finds its intended receiver anymore; all of these misguided soliloquies end up in an incoherent cacophony.

In general, like science fiction, the fantastic is a tool that enables us to broach the great anguish found in the material. In these texts we find the same themes that are developed throughout the corpus, but they are pushed beyond the rational, the reasonable; thus they form an excellent introduction to the discussion that follows: the hardening of social relationships; the decline of solidarity; the difficulties of intimate relationships; the treachery of experts; the impotence of institutions. The only

6. Contemporary French sculptor known for his large sculptures of compressed metals and other industrial materials.—TRANS.

glimmer of hope resides in art in general and music in particular.

To conclude with the temporal framework of the synopses, we should note that all of the texts unfold within a short period of time: as if the characters find themselves plunged into a world that is both deprived of a past and lacking a future. And what is true of the collection's relationship to time is also true of the individual relationships: in their personal lives the characters also exist in brief spans of time. The accent is deliberately placed on the present moment. Their past is presented to them in an abrupt and discontinuous way, in the form of flashbacks, but never as a series of organized memories that might form a continuous thread and provide an anchoring or a mobilizing experience. Their future is not guided by a specific plan.

Relationships are characterized by this instantaneousness: they are encounters that are formed and unformed in the course of a text. They can go quite far and deeply engage the various protagonists, but they are rarely inscribed in the long term.

Relationships are characterized by quick leaps to intimacy with others that short-circuit all the socially ritualized stages in the progress of a relationship: open to diversity, characters seize opportunities for encounters, but bonds come apart as quickly as they are formed. This has an impact on the type of plots that are developed. There are, for example, very few stories that center on the development of a relationship that assumes a portrayal of a long period of time and a summoning of shared memories: only twelve stories of people who find each other after being separated by circumstances in life and only seven stories of revenge. There are also few tales dealing with long-ruminated

Table 2. Duration of the Action

	Historical Fiction (%)	All Texts (%)
A few hours	12	35
A few days	36	43
Several hours	48	18
A lifetime	4	3

conflicts: no dramas à la Bergman, no couples torn apart by domestic quarrels. No families à la Mauriac. The privilege granted to immediacy preserves relationships from the risks of decay. The lives of most of the characters thus unfold at an expeditious, choppy, broken rhythm, very similar to the writing of the synopses themselves, in which actions occur in rapid succession. These characteristics are, moreover, often underscored by the authors themselves in the introductory notes on visual style that authors give to specify the tone of their screenplays: "the rhythm is rapid, similar to a modern rendering of images, to the pace of music videos." The spasmodic prose of the screenplays gives one the impression of watching the characters move around in a jerky way, at a jarring pace, as if they were on a dance floor under the beams of a strobe light.

THE GEOGRAPHICAL FRAMEWORK

The proximity of historical time is mirrored by that of geographical space. An overwhelming majority of screenplays take place in France. The authors have no taste for the exotic. Those few scripts that are set abroad are, moreover, also often works of historical fiction: Cambodia, Senegal, Venezuela, the Middle East, New York, Los Angeles. In these cases the focal point is therefore both historically and geographically distant.

Eastern bloc countries are the exception, however, and have inspired a certain number of projects. The fall of the Berlin Wall, the raising of the Iron Curtain, have inspired texts that speak not of the internal upheavals of Eastern bloc countries,

Table 3. Geographical Settings

	%
Foreign country	9
Paris	32
Suburbs of Paris	14
Other City in France	30
Rural area	4
En route	4
Unspecified	7

but of the renewed flow of people between the two European blocs. There are two variants of this theme: the departure of new migrants to the West, or the return of former emigrants to the East. Thus we see in a comedy for example how the entire Tchitchitoff family launches on a conquest of the West "where every coveted object is ready to be picked like a flower," at 50 mph in a Fiat 126 overflowing with parcels. They end up in a supermarket–department store that they will not be able to leave, since the children have eaten a chocolate bar that the parents can't pay for. They therefore settle in the store, eating in the food aisles, sleeping in the furniture department, reading in the book section, cooking in the household appliance department, feasting on televised images, under the astonished eyes of the French customers and to the great satisfaction of the manager of the store, who is delighted with the publicity he is attracting from their presence *(Vous n'en reviendrez pas!)*.

The journey might also be made in the opposite direction, and several synopses tell of a return to the East by exiles who were living in the West: a family is bringing back the coffin of their grandfather on the roof of their car; their grandfather was a former White Russian whose children want to bury him in St. Petersburg *(Paris/Saint-Pétersbourg)*. A woman goes to Rumania to look for a person with whom she had spent many hours talking during a train trip more than twenty years earlier; the postcard she sent to the old address "like a message in a bottle," finally reaches the addressee, and the two women meet again. A text written by a young woman born in Bucharest and living in Paris evokes a reunion with her parents after years of separation. But in fact, in one way or another, and regardless of the direction of the journey, these texts always end with a reciprocal disillusionment.

Let us return to the majority of the texts: we are in France, sometimes in a village (usually located south of the Loire), sometimes in a small city (usually in the north), most often in the suburbs of Paris. Often the geographical setting is not specified: it is then a large, unrecognizable city. Setting the story in an environment close at hand obviously has an impact on the content of the tale itself. It does not resemble a documentary project. There is no question of using a plot to explore geographical or human diversity, uncommon landscapes, a variety of forms of architecture, habitats, clothing, customs, food. There are no exotic minutia. We are, on the contrary, in a world that we know well, monotonous and familiar, at the opposite side of the one visited by Milou and Tintin.[7]

An imagined space is always related to an imagined social reality. Every setting is emblematic of a specific social category: small cities provide an opportunity to speak of the provincial bourgeoisie; the suburbs are the territory of immigrants, the countryside that of peasants; Paris is the world of the media, advertising, and panhandlers. In the very simplified representation of the social world that is at work in the synopses, each category has its own territory, of which the category is in some way the symbol.

We cannot discuss the frameworks within which the plots take place without mentioning that the authors complain about them: they find their settings ugly. Their characters develop within spoiled environments. "A dark street with walls covered with graffiti and vulgarities; crumbling buildings, broken work site fences, wrecked cars. Two punks are enjoying sticking a star-shaped blade into what was once the front door of a building" (*Les terrains vagues*). The suburbs described are not those of bungalows with little fenced-in backyards and flowers; they are the suburbs of high-rise projects and iron bars, vacant lots, and graffiti. The suburbs that simmer. We read the reflections of Inspector Picot, "who through the window of his patrol car watches the procession of dark suburban landscapes that to him appear as the dead-ends of urban development and the cul-de-sacs of social progress" (*Rap Side Story*). This vision is reinforced by specific climatic characteristics: suburban skies are

7. Main characters in the popular *Tintin* comic book series.—TRANS.

always gray and hazy. It rains a lot in the suburbs. Likewise, deindustrialization gives former mining areas a desolate look, as in "Saint-Rémy-du-Nord, a small provincial city with houses scattered between the abandoned factories and fields dotted with abandoned dump sites; unemployment and boredom" (*Ratonnade*).

But rural areas are no better off. There are no bucolic pathways fragrant with rosemary and humming with the song of cicadas on summer nights. The countryside portrayed in the texts is always threatened. It is caught between the risks of being abandoned (*La sirène des Pyrénées*) and those of invading modernity (tourist complexes or oil refineries, highway interchanges, factories to treat radioactive waste): "October. Night falls. A peasant, Bernard, forty years old, brown beard and hair, calls his animals. His cows return in single file to the farm that is surrounded by a few fields, encircled by shopping centers, a state highway, factories, and a beltway" (*Chemin de terre*). The country is therefore much too unstable to provide an imaginary refuge in the face of the vicissitudes of urban life. The image of the village, so positive at the end of the 1970s when the nascent ecological movements were associated with the theme of a return to the land, is not at all present in the synopses: village life is hostile; knowledge of one's neighbors is no longer synonymous with conviviality, but with social control. In many of the texts the peasants represented are archaic and hostile. They show kindness or simple humanity only in works of historical fiction, with the receding of time. Isn't this attitude just one more expression among others of a refusal to believe that somewhere, elsewhere, there exist enchanted alternatives? Just as the authors refuse a nostalgic reference to a mythical past, they do not allow themselves a calming representation of a harmonious rural life. They no longer have any illusions. We are therefore led into a world without recourse.

To conclude, let us note the large number of journeys represented: many of the texts portray characters in motion, going from one place to another: artists looking for social advancement go to Paris; women in search of themselves leave the capital; delinquents make their escape; fringe elements go for walks;

the middle class goes on vacation. Ebb and flow, circulation, wandering.

THE SOCIOLOGICAL FRAMEWORK

Before launching the characters into their adventures, we should mention a few facts about the social worlds in which they evolve.

Table 4. Age of Main Characters

	%
Children	11
15–25 years	16
25–35 years	55
Mature adult	10
Elderly	8

NOTE: In order to determine who the main character was, I started with the plot. When the text presented several protagonists of apparently equivalent importance, I relied on the summary the author provided in the application forms, and on the ranking the author established among the characters.

There are very few births (eight), although the number of living children is high. There is usually only one child in a family: there are scarcely any large families (except in the historical fictions and in texts that portray traditional middle-class families), and what is more interesting, there are no families that have been reassembled following successive divorces, i.e., today's large families (only seven screenplays).

Table 5. Gender of Hero

Male	65%
Female	35%

The death rate is high. In this regard the difference between police stories and psychological dramas is that in the first category death occurs at the beginning of the story, whereas in the second it occurs at the time of the denouement. The high mortality rate of the population is connected to the high number of violent deaths: accidents, homicides, suicides. There are not very many common illnesses, cancers, cardiovascular disease. Very little AIDS, which clearly remains a taboo subject: only two stories make it the focal point of their plots (a nurse and an infected prostitute), otherwise a few infected characters mentioned briefly in the course of a story. On the whole, characters suffer more from psychological troubles than from physical illness. Thus the use of tranquilizers, drugs (ten texts), but especially alcohol. Finding refuge in alcohol appears as the constant, primary solution to the difficulties of life.

As we have seen, an urban population predominates, and residential mobility is high. If we now look at connections to work, we note a large proportion of the unemployed. There are basically few heroes who work. There are many unemployed, idle young people, the elderly, panhandlers, and vagrants. There is much irregular work: work is a rare commodity. It no longer serves as the foundation for one's identity.

If we look only at the main characters who exercise a profession and divide them up according to socioprofessional categories, we obtain information that is in fact not very enlightening for a description of the internal world of the synopses.

However, this list of professions is very similar to the listing established by the surveys of the Société Française d'Enquêtes et de Sondages to examine the perceived usefulness or the prestige of certain professions. There is a true connection between

Table 6. The Hero's Work

Without a profession[a]	36%
Exercising a profession, but existence is portrayed outside of that profession	38%
Film existence coincides with the exercise of a profession	26%

NOTE: These figures were obtained after omitting works of historical fiction and of science fiction.

[a]Retired, homeless, vagrant, unemployed, child, etc.

Table 7. The Professional Landscape

Farmer	8%
Artisan, merchant, head of company	23%
Executive, higher intellectual profession, artist	39%
Midlevel profession	7%
Employee	2%
Laborer	2%

the two ways of constructing reality. This phenomenon is very enlightening as to the way in which information circulates: we can easily see how the authors borrow the ingredients for their synopses from other sources. They import into their projects characters that are made available to them by the ambient culture, finding support in the fact that the characters' importance has already been established somewhere else, for other reasons, and they know that their audience knows it. Their characters may appear in opinion polls, in news items, in the press, in the world of comic books, in television news shows, film, literature, etc. The authors then allow them to convey a *different* and unique significance. But they are bolstered by shared common cultural resources.[8]

8. The following list was made up by SOFRES based on surveys on the prestige of professions. It is not the order of classification that interests us here, but the *nomenclature used,* which reflects a certain *concordance in the establishment of a scale of professional visibility* with the choice of characters made by the screenwriters. At the top of the list are scientific researchers (72 percent of the French grant them a great deal of prestige), doctors (58 percent), nurses (43 percent), engineers (42 percent), judges (39 percent), heads of companies (35 percent), writers (29 percent), teachers (29 percent), sports figures (29 percent), workers (28 percent), lawyers (27 percent), farmers (23 percent), officers (23 percent), prefects (22 percent), film actors (21 percent), journalists (19 percent), businessmen (17 percent), television announcers (17 percent), priests (17 percent), politicians (16 percent), bankers (15 percent), merchants (14 percent), bureaucrats (9 percent), advertisers (9 percent) (in *L'état de l'opinion,* presented by Olivier Duhamel and Jérôme Jaffré [Paris, 1991]). In the 1992 edition French people were asked to grade each of the following categories or professions from 1 to 10 based on their usefulness. The various professions were classified in the following order: nurses, workers, doctors, teachers in primary or secondary education, farmers, engineers, university professors, mailmen, policemen, heads of companies, small merchants, magistrates, bank employees, executives in accounting and financial enterprises, artists, journalists, commercial executives, priests and preachers, high-level bureaucrats, deputies, prostitutes (Olivier Duhamel and Jérôme Jaffré, *L'état de l'opinion* [Paris, 1992]).

The decline of industrial society is echoed and amplified: the working class is practically nonexistent. There are, however, merchants, artisans, low-level bureaucrats, and, not surprisingly, many policemen; professionals (doctors, architects, lawyers, nurses); a few executives, some industrialists. There are very few elected officials: the political personnel represented are situated at the local level, and not in the national arena. Professions in communication, fashion, and advertising appear often. These are the professions that occupy the most prestigious positions, having replaced a decadent aristocracy at the top of the social hierarchy (an aristocracy that is confined to fantastic texts and endowed with strange behaviors) and a superconventional middle class, hardened by its principles and clutching to its privileges. If there are few professional burglars, there are many small-time delinquents, pimps, dealers, prostitutes. And above all so many artists.

What is striking in the social representation in the universe of the synopses is that the characters are not defined by their adherence to a specific class (with the exception of the middle class and farmers who are clearly identified as such). For most characters, the exercise of a profession (or the fact of being unemployed) occurs within a social void. There is no longer any trace of a class struggle. No discourse on injustice, no organized denunciation of inequality, no stories supported by a clear ideological agenda. Nor do we find groups that traditionally take responsibility for this type of discourse: there are no political parties, no unions, no small militant groups. Associations are rare, and most are taken an extremely dim view of, which demonstrates a great distrust of all forms of adherence to a group. Yet this doesn't mean that the world presented is considered just: on the contrary, the social order is seen as fundamentally perverted, since each individual who has a bit of power redirects it for his own profit, and because, on the other hand, all those who are proponents of an alternative are excluded or marginalized. But this representation never ends up in a political perspective: no hero proposes a plan to overthrow this social order. *Society is so lacking in cohesion that it seems impossible to shake up its foundations.* In some of the synopses we see acts of terrorism, but they are isolated, sporadic acts, undertaken within a logic of the absurd. Consequently, the only solutions the characters come up with are of an individual nature: to try to escape from one's condition by oneself, by suddenly becoming rich, and as soon as possible.

PLOTS

There is therefore a certain amount of agreement in the internal characteristics of the world as it is described by the authors of the synopses. This consensus bears not only on the temporal, geographical, and sociological framework in which the characters develop, but also on the types of adventures they are likely to have. In fact, these adventures can be grouped into a limited number of characteristic plots that then unfold in many various ways: only *twenty thematic elements are needed to produce almost all the stories described in the corpus.*[9]

In fact, in a work of fiction, the author seeks to reach the audience by evoking their interest. He therefore attempts to have direct access to their emotions. To achieve this he will "pack" his material with meaning. But what is very complicated is that depending on the story the author has chosen to tell, *meaning is not imprinted in the same way.* Sometimes it bears on the character (homeless panhandlers, a developer, an old man). Sometimes it is in the setting (Eastern bloc countries, the countryside). It may also be in the context (the universe of messengers, the world of advertising), or in the direction given to the plot. The author takes an extremely conventional story, a search for one's father—the theme of choice in popular litera-

---

9. Each synopsis was only counted once. To determine the main subject of the plot, I relied on the content of the text, on the summary provided by the author at the end of his or her application, on the note of intent that usually accompanied the project, and on the telephone conversations I had with the two hundred authors whose texts I was citing. This was both the first stage of my work and the final one. I reworked the stacks to do the final counting only when the entire analysis had been completed.

ture of the nineteenth century—but changes its meaning: reunions no longer lead to happiness, but to disappointment, etc.
However, the author counts on our competence as ordinary
viewers, accustomed to existing in the same referential universe,
to understand his intentions. He assumes we will be able to see
that specific murder as a convention, *that* stabbing as no more
than a device, but the character of *this* man, on the contrary,
is where our attention should be drawn.[10]

The breakdown of synopses according to plot should not
be viewed as a catalog, but rather as a succession of nuclei
around which similar texts gravitate. The texts are, moreover,
themselves crossed by intersecting thematics: what forms the
central plot of one story might be found again in another but
in a subordinate manner, as a miniplot that accompanies the
principal story, just as settings and characters reappear in various capacities. *These are the fragments that by recurrently appearing in one text and another join the synopses together.* The
list may appear a bit enigmatic, but its content will be clarified
in the course of the present analysis. While being precise it has
the advantage of covering almost all the material, and of giving a
numbered indication of the relative importance of the different
subjects found in the corpus itself. The list does not coincide
exactly with the themes that will be discussed (even if it covers
them in part) in that it is organized around the *main theme* of
the plot, whereas a displaying of the overall contents is based
on *all of the figures* that appear in a recurrent fashion (a disagreeable character is rarely the main subject of a story).[11] In
general, when a figure appears in a secondary role, he or she

10. This aspect, which is essential for an understanding of the approach adopted,
is developed in the section on methodology.

11. For example: real estate developers never constitute the main subject of a
plot. They appear among the elderly when they want to tear down a retirement
home, in the threatened countryside when they have plans for tourist developments,
sometimes among the "couples in crisis" when the story concerns the purchase of
a badly built house from a developer who is presented as the instigator of the
breakup; and most often among immigrants when developers have built suburbs or
considered tearing them down. The elderly are in the category of the "old tonics"
when they are cheerful, but included in mismatched friendships when they are
wise, etc.

Table 8. Breakdown of Synopses by Main Subject of Plots

	Number of Texts
1. Historical fiction	77
Scholarly	
Heroic	
2. Science fiction	24
Genetic manipulation	
Ecological disaster	
3. The fantastic	26
The glaucous supernatural	
Autonomy of technical objects	
4. Police dramas	148
Psychiatric criminality	
Sexual relations with unknown persons are dangerous	
Psychiatrists are even worse	
Sociological delinquency	
Technological fraud	
International terrorism, drug trafficking, espionage	
Human-interest stories	
5. Eastern bloc countries	19
Departure or return: itinerary of disappointment	
6. Threatened countryside	28
How can it be saved?	
7. Immigrants	37
First generation or impossible integration	
Suburbs, violence, projects, North Africans	
8. Lively old folks or a love of life	33
9. Film in which a child is the hero	52
Childhood and the marvelous	
Super-intelligent child (computer science, etc.)	
10. The handicapped and a passion for beauty	22
11. Art	69
Small jobs and artistic sweatshop	
Splendor and solitude of the artist	
Music or fusion	
12. Media stories: the invaders	38
13. Families	36
Rivalry between indistinct generations	
Incestuous deviations	
Parents-children; brothers-sisters	
14. Fatherhood	37
Father in search of child	
Child in search of father	
15. Couples in crisis	16
Overbearing woman	
Wife-swapping, foursomes	
16. Impossible loves	16
Truly major impediments	
17. Adolescent loves	28
18. Mismatched friendships	20
19. Wandering and solitude	35
20. Deconstructing the subject	22
Unclassifiable	19
Professional Locales	13
Total	**817**

is introduced as having the same characteristics as when he or she is the main subject of the plot. It is this principle of continuity that justifies the approach used here. The one exception, however, is where the media itself is a theme. The theme itself has inspired benevolent synopses stamped with a certain goodwill, whereas media professionals are the objects of much more hostile treatment when they appear within the course of the texts. (This is perhaps because the authors deemed it preferable not to send a television station a project that treats its world too harshly.)

It is also interesting to note the subjects that are dealt with: only two texts focus on homosexuality. Three synopses are devoted to the theme of sports (one of which was ultimately chosen: *Le poids du corps*). Religion is brought up primarily in works of historical fiction. Of the synopses situated in the present time, only four made a priest, a monk, or a minister the main character of their plots (in these cases, they are always positive characters). There are only six stories of crimes of passion. Twelve texts aim to describe a specific professional milieu by means of a standard plot (a department store, a flower shop, a foreign-exchange window, a window at a social security office). If some topics appear infrequently, this is undoubtedly related to the personal backgrounds of the authors (they appear more interested, for example, in the artistic ambitions of their characters than in their athletic performances), or perhaps the result of a certain type of self-censorship linked to their assumptions about the expectations of television stations. But in any event, from our perspective here, it is less the motivations of the authors that matters than the forms they have chosen to adopt and that have taken shape in the corpus.

Up to now we have largely emphasized the common elements that connect the texts. We must not interpret this emphasis as a reflection of the never-ending criticism of the lack of imagination among authors. Such criticism misses the sociological dimension of television production: it is precisely because the same subjects appear again and again, redeveloped, reworked by each author in a specific way, that they are so interesting. This guarantees that they have a collective dimension and therefore participate in a common culture, somewhat in the manner of the Balinese villages studied by Clifford Geertz:

> As more and more villages are studied it soon becomes clear that a relatively small set of basic elements is involved. (. . .) But though the number and type of elements are thus fairly quickly discovered the possible forms they can take and the ways in which they can unite with the other elements are not. (. . .) The process of investigating Balinese village organization, in a typological sense, is therefore a process of progressive delimitation of the structural possibilities inherent in a set of fundamental social elements. What one derives is not a typical village in either the lowest common denominator or representative unit sense, but a differentiated and multidimensional social space within which actual Balinese village organizations are necessarily distributed. One discovers more and more what shapes a village can take and still be distinctively Balinese.[12]

A SPIRALING CRISIS

Now that we have determined some of the elements at play in the material to be studied, it might be possible to get at the common issues that appear to unify them. Indeed, if all the texts seemed to "hold together," it was clearly because they shared common elements, because certain settings, characters, objects, dialogue, events, and plots appeared again and again, forcing the reader to take notice. But it was also because a set of underlying themes seemed to run through the collection, from text to text, as if a single process permeated the entire universe of the synopses.

There are three types of stage settings in this imagined world that correspond moreover to rather different writing styles. The first is that of the *social* setting. Rather stereotyped characters encounter each other here. The heroes, either vic-

12. Clifford Geertz, "Form and Variation in Balinese Village Structure," *American Anthropologist* 61 (1959): 991–1012.

tims or those living in the margins of society, are confronted
with adversaries who are clearly identified by the place they
occupy in society.

The second setting depicts *private life:* the characters are
simply ordinary beings who find themselves faced with people
who are much like them and who inspire neither camaraderie
nor rejection. Their sociological environment becomes indis-
tinct, their social position no longer has much importance, their
profession is a pretext. They shed their social attributes to be
defined essentially by psychological characteristics. Plots are
knit around the issues of personal relationships. Danger comes
with intimate relationships.

The framework of the third setting is the *individual* himself,
faced with his solitude. Society has come undone, all relationships are impossible, and the individual himself no longer exists:
he is a fragmented being looking for himself, pure interiority
drawn by a search for aesthetic accomplishments on a solitary
journey.

The same spiraling effect pulls the characters from the most
external forms of social life to the heart of individual unique-
ness. It is as if they were caught in a process that led to a generalized crisis of all forms of interpersonal connection: a crisis of
the social bond, a crisis of the familial bond, a crisis of the bond
that holds a personality together. At question throughout these
texts is the individual's ability to maintain a relationship.
Plunged into a world of instability and uncertainty, caught up
in a logic of suspicion of others and of self-doubt, the characters
in the synopses are forced to manage not a material crisis, but
a moral one. They are plunged into a world threatened by atom-
ization, in which relationships seem impossible to maintain because they are no longer regulated by an external order that
would guarantee some kind of permanence and allow some kind
of cohesion. In fact, everything occurs as if the characters were
beginning to discover that *the crisis of institutions is gradually
making any form of interpersonal bond impossible.*[13] We can

13. The French word used here and throughout the text is *lien,* which can mean
"bond," "tie," or "relationship." The word *bond* seems best to capture the author's
meaning.—Trans.

then see very well the contradiction with which they are confronted. On the one hand, they are still fixated on past ideologies of freedom and continue to find that any form of externally imposed order is impossible to accept (institutions are unjust and constraining), but on the other hand, their social and interpersonal lives become unmanageable, the void created by the absence of regulations producing a general feeling of instability that gives rise to cynicism. But since any return to the past seems impossible, the rigidity of old structures being definitively unbearable, and because any form of regulation appears improbable, since no kind of order could be considered as legitimate, they find themselves confronted with a feeling of powerlessness. In the face of this new form of fatalism, the only viable reactions are retreating into an aestheticizing contemplation of the ugliness of the world, or adopting a position of humor that shows that, if one has indeed understood that the world is thus and that one can change nothing in it, there at least remains the compensation of knowing that one is not the dupe of it. Such is the overall set of values that appears to inform the entire corpus, giving it its unity, its very current character, but also its fundamentally pessimistic tone.

This model appears quite simple, but it did not come to me all at once. It was by reading and rereading the synopses that it gradually took shape: I started by looking at the characters, the characteristics that were attributed to them, the positions they occupied within a plot, and the positioning of that plot within the entire corpus. I based my approach on the feeling I had that all these synopses were connected and that they evoked the same crisis, in an attempt to identify the nature of that crisis and to find a logical form of presentation that would enable me to arrange all thousand texts around a single axis.

I therefore tested out a number of patterns, one after the other. The first revolved around the idea that what characterized the universe of the synopses was the process of exclusion that ran through it, a process through which positive characters were systematically relegated to the margins. This enabled me to organize the presentation of the texts dealing with the inner workings of social organization; however, it didn't work for the intimist texts. Yet I had the feeling that there was real continuity between the social and the individual. The second revolved around the idea of pessimism. In each of the three settings mentioned above, there was in fact that same process of excluding any form of positiveness (the positive characters were relegated to the margins, good feelings to limbo, the individual himself, disintegrated). But I lacked any support to argue this position: was this collection of texts truly more gloomy than any other? Isn't fiction always an expression of unhappiness? How could I develop this theme if I didn't have any points for comparison? The third, centered around the notion of a crisis of bonds, appeared to be useful, but it remained descriptive. Each time, I reorganized the entire presentation in order to arrange all of the texts around the new axis I had chosen because it was here that the enigma of the material lay: if all of these texts appeared to speak of the same thing, we must certainly be able to find what that thing was. Indeed, this principle of ordering formed the very object of my research. I looked for it a long time, and finally, I found it: the crisis of bonds was *a consequence* of the crisis of institutions. Out of that notion everything fit together fine. This solution had an explanatory dimension since it established a causal relationship between those two elements. It shed light on the strange atmosphere that permeated the corpus. It enabled me to account for all of the texts. It established continuity between the three areas of action. It integrated the screenplays that were the exception as well as those that were in the majority. It even incorporated the works of historical fiction, which, through their differences, found a place along the *continuum*. It therefore met all the stated objectives. Consequently, it is from this perspective that I will now discuss the body of material.

Two

Social Bonds

The world of the synopses is a world in crisis. We have the feeling that society has come undone. It is simultaneously anomic and ruled by the laws of the jungle. Characters attempt to shape themselves and to survive in a hostile universe. To understand better what this hostility is made of we will begin by looking at the main characters and at the way in which they are described.

There are indeed a certain number of characters that seem to travel from one text to another, bringing ever-similar characteristics with them. In certain texts they appear in a primary role, and the plot centers around them; in other texts they appear as secondary characters. But even when they make only a brief appearance in a synopsis, they are described along relatively similar lines, have the same material or symbolic attributes, the same qualities, the same failings.

My approach was therefore made up of four steps. First, it was important to identify the characters that appeared most frequently by actually counting them, then to determine, from the attributes bestowed upon the characters, what type of values they represented. I then formed groups by combining main characters with other characters that were described similarly, had the same characteristics, or perhaps intervened in a similar manner in a story. Finally, starting from these large categories, I attempted to perceive how this imagined world was organized and to identify the malaises that ran through it.

Some of these emblematic figures will be presented: policemen, real estate developers, and doctors on the one hand; immigrants, elderly people, children, the handicapped, and artists, on the other. Each of these figures serves as the rather simple embodiment of a guiding principle. They also serve to identify the tensions that weigh on that imagined world and produce the disintegration of social bonds: in looking at the lives of policemen we see the impotency of institutions sketched before us; looking at the developer, we see the defection of bosses; at doctors, the betrayal of experts; at immigrants, the failure of the integration of minorities; at the handicapped and artists, a promotion of aesthetic values; at the elderly, a yearning for meaningful relationships. Thus appear these fundamental logical couples that structure this universe of representations and allow the precise identification of the concrete form of the crisis in this imaginary world.

Each figure enables us to create a larger whole, for they are emblematic of a group. Each figure gathers a certain number of people under its banner who would surely be quite shocked to find themselves put together: alongside the doctors there are of course lawyers, notaries, and other professionals, but there are also scientific researchers, hairdressers, personal trainers, pimps, dealers, evil nurses, people who practice spiritism: all those who use their abilities to exercise direct power over the body or mind of others. With the police we find customs officers, educators, professors, social workers, ticket collectors, international bureaucrats, priests. With the handicapped, a crowd of actors, musicians, singers, dancers, and ordinary people, all those who are drawn toward a fulfillment of aesthetic ideals. There aren't very many people grouped with the elderly, with the exception of children.

Let us first look at one of the most classic figures of televised fiction: the policeman. Since police dramas are the fodder for prime-time programming, they have provided us with a number of models for fictional policemen: there are some who are very clever, very effective, very satanical, very repressive—like the policeman and former criminal Vidocq, Commissaire Maigret, Navarro, Commissaire Moulin, Nestor Burma. But the policemen in our synopses do not seem to have come from any of these lineages.

THE POWERLESSNESS OF INSTITUTIONS
Policemen

> The inside of Inspector Leon's office is just as pitiful as the outside. The blue tiled floor is worn, and the walls are filthy with years of grimy handprints. The chairs are rickety, and the lamp sheds little light. Leon enters and, glancing in the mirror, sees his tired eyes and his five o'clock shadow. He shuts the door. He heads to the other side of his desk, sits down, and lights a cigarette. (*Léon*)

And in fact, inspectors quite often resemble their place of work. It is interesting that the physical descriptions are always similar: badly shaven, an air of fatigue, tired eyes. Yet these policemen are not Colombo's younger brothers: as far as the wrinkled-raincoat look is concerned, they are still fairly similar, but the essential difference is that they do not catch guilty criminals. The policemen of the synopses are not supercops.

They are often retired, or have in fact become bums—such as the one who fought against alcoholism, but finally lost the battle. ("He ends up in Nanterre House, a former prison where they put panhandlers, alcoholics, and other social rejects when they are picked up in public places. He lived like that for fifteen years, sometimes locked up in that semi-imprisoning world, sometimes free, living off of handouts, sleeping in the street.") But it also happens that some policemen do a complete turnaround and quite simply become crooks. The one thing they never do is fulfill their function of maintaining order: in the suburbs they are happy to check IDs at random. In the police dramas that were submitted they are never the ones who solve crimes: it is always amateurs, journalists, or children. And if a policeman ever discovers the perpetrator of a crime, he always has a good reason to let him or her go: it's a former girlfriend, the woman he loved, the one he's falling in love with. Or, as for Julia Zimmerman, the guilty one is Ric, her brother.

Pesé, compté, divisé

A flashing light; it always begins with a flashing light. Afterward there are the screams, the sheets stained with blood, the flashing cameras of newspaper reporters, the body that's carried out. Standing in a corner, Commissaire Julia Zimmerman looks at the scene, smoking a cigarette. She's wearing an aviator-style jacket, and her blunt-cut blond hair sparkles in the rain. Flora, the tall Brazilian transvestite who works next door, saw nothing, heard nothing. As usual. Julia is tired. She is approaching forty without much optimism. She is in a good position to know that life pulls no punches. Anything can happen to anyone, anytime. Even in a little provincial city, a summer retreat lying dormant in the winter. For example, this guy who began to kill. And to kill in a particularly horrible way, as if some deaths were more beautiful than others. As if she didn't have enough to worry about.

It is difficult to be a representative of the maintaining of public order since the notion of order itself has been so terribly altered. The police in the synopses are unjust when they act, ignoble when they do not intervene. But this is not really their own fault, because they are dealing with very ambiguous demands. They are expected to be able to insure our safety better—and this is not a luxury, for the world of the synopses is extremely dangerous—but at the same time to be more understanding toward the guilty. To be more understanding while being firmer. It is up to them to figure out how to walk the middle ground between the paradoxical expectations of cultural liberalism and the rise of security-minded ideologies.

If we look more closely, we note that a policeman's problem is intrinsically linked to the evolution of the forms of criminality. The story of the carefully prepared bank robbery that kept us breathless in front of our television sets for many evenings, with its preparations, its sophisticated tools, its cleverness, its unexpected turns, is not represented in the synopses. It is noteworthy that once again the issue of the representation of time is raised here: the difficulty of creating well-developed projects is not unrelated to the disappearance of this type of plot. Nor are policemen confronted with the milieu of well-run delinquency, with its rules, its rituals, and its loyalties, which might evoke Chicago of the 1930s as well as the local variations of the Mafia. This nonetheless does not imply that policemen have joined the ranks of evildoers, following a traditional reversal of roles: big-hearted thieves, those who steal from the rich to give to the poor, are essentially absent from the corpus. There are a few, of course, in the works of historical fiction and some in texts set in the present time, but which make explicit reference to the past—a character is named Robin of the Hoods, another Mandrin of the Twentieth Century, still another Arsèn(a) Lupin(ette)—or appear in a parodic fashion, in plots whose beneficiaries are tame animals. (*Les arnaqueuses* are "pretty young women, sexy, lively, full of charm and humor" who, in order to finance their society for the protection of animals carry out large-scale robberies against those who abuse animals.) The protection of animals as a truly positive element is significant for this second-level culture that permeates the texts, but it also shows, for reasons we are beginning to see, how difficult it is in the world of the synopses to propose a mobilization for more human causes.

Three types of crimes appear in the synopses: the first are sociologized *thefts*, delinquency of frustration. The second are *murders*, the psychiatric crimes of the irresponsible. The third, *frauds*, the technowork of experts. This means that in every instance the problem that the police have to deal with is reformulated in terms that take it beyond their realm of competence.

The police are dealing with sociological delinquency, one engendered by a gulf that has never been wider between the availability of consumer goods, the solicitations of advertising

as orchestrated by the media, and a lack of financial resources.[1]
Young people help themselves in supermarkets, in grocery
stores, they steal a motorcycle, a scooter, a car for the evening.
("He was arrested for shoplifting. 'They shouldn't have put all
that in front of me,' he answered.") It is a chance delinquency,
much too fleeting to be the object of a plot: theft is rather presented as just another part of life. Faced with a rise in this extremely commonplace delinquency of frustration, it is clear just
how insufficient are the traditionally repressive methods that
have been used to deal with it.

La vie en HLM

The group enters a grocery store. They yell at each other
to find out what they will buy. The grocer, appalled to see
them all come in together, hurries to head them off, and
seeing them touch everything, he watches their every move,
expecting disaster. Delighted to see them pay, he then starts
giving them advice on easy dishes to prepare, and jokes with
them. He disappears into a trap door and returns, out of
breath, with some boxes. One of the young men can't help
stealing something, anyway. The old man is smiling, but is
relieved when they finally leave.

Taupe secret

She's blind as a bat, speaks three languages, and is out of
work. He is rather handsome, dances divinely, a waiter by
day, a burglar by night. She has only one goal: to find a job
where she can use her three languages. He has only one
goal: to score a big hit, and then, so-long espressos and
beers, hello sun—he wants to open a nightclub and dance!
Unbeknownst to them they live in the same neighborhood.
Having nothing really in common, they shouldn't meet. And
yet they do.

1. François Dubet, *La galère: Jeunes en survie* (Paris, 1987).

One evening, to make a little money, Agnès babysits for the Dubosques—the very same Dubosques that Sylvain has chosen to rob that evening. He tries to gag her, she resists, pulls off the scarf that is hiding his face. He escapes, but the next day she recognizes him in the corner café.

The second form of delinquency found in the synopses is a criminality of psychiatric origin. Mental illness plays an important role here. It is therefore not surprising that most of the crimes are committed by deeply disturbed people, which is, moreover, the thematics of choice in American thrillers. In a psychological portrait of the assassins, authors very often mention the existence of a childhood trauma: the guilty carry around a secret traumatic wound that causes them to kill, and there is nothing that can halt the process. This trauma demands an atonement quite different from traditional revenge in that it is not the guilty who are punished, but the innocent who pay. The experiences of the past do not accumulate in the killer's memory; they are stocked in his subconscious, inciting him to plan unexpected uprisings against arbitrary victims. This logic is endlessly repeated: if the person who commits violence or a rape has his head filled with flashbacks of his childhood wounds and his past traumas, the same was true with his initial aggressor. And somewhat later his victim, perhaps in another synopsis, will in turn take up the weapon of the crime: the spiral of irresponsibility thus unwinds through history, justifying anonymous aggressions against unknown victims.

The third type of crimes that police encounter is the fraudulence of experts, connected to the possession of specific knowledge. They thus find themselves confronted with terribly intelligent swindlers who are often highly educated, who master the current technology, notably computer science, to perfection, have high-level scientific and technical competency, knowledge of the law, an artistic expertise. The rise in this form of astute delinquency, that of an expert who redirects his unique expertise for criminal purposes, is also very disarming for the police.

This explains why the mysteries in the proposed police fictions are solved by scholars, archaeologists, engineers, journalists, museum curators, and even children.

Within this general context of the changing forms of delinquency, it is not very surprising that the police are a bit obsolete. We now understand better why they retire, quit their jobs, or turn to a life of crime themselves.

But we discover that they are not alone in their dilemma. In one way or another all professionals who work in an institution find themselves in the same situation. Looking over the synopses, if we consider all the characters who are employees representing an institution, we note that they are all confronted with the same type of difficulties: social workers sink into alcoholism (*Bébé-cloche*); social security employees are very shopworn behind their desks (*Le bureau*); the firemen who remain full of good intentions would be completely ready to put out a fire, if they could only hook up their hoses ("No one knows why, but they're shooting out fire. They have turned into flamethrowers"); teachers are depressed; prison directors are in league with the prisoners (*Une trajectoire de papillon*); judges no longer go to the courthouse (*Clair obscur*); lighthouse watchmen desert their posts; out-of-work customs officials, whose wives have left them, abandoned by their dog, constantly empty their reserves of contraband alcohol (*Les douaniers*). As for priests, they find unusual solutions to the problems of housing projects in crisis (*L'argent fait le bonheur*). And what can be said of the mailman who wakes up one morning unable to go on his route:

L'Entrave

To find yourself weighed down by a ball and chain puts you in a stressful, even absurd, situation, especially if you are a mailman and it happens to you while getting on your bicycle.

This is what happens to Simon Bièvre, a mailman who apparently is without problems.

Stupor and panic gone, he has to get out of sight of passersby, his freedom and security depend on it.

Then get rid of this really cumbersome object.

Getting out of sight of others is very difficult, even in an apartment: the windows aren't secure, the curtains sometimes let some sunshine in.

The bathroom?

Not if the window looks out over the roof, where his dog is used to running around, whose barking might alert the neighbors.

The entry way?

Perhaps. But only if his door shuts perfectly tight and doesn't let any light come in between the floor and the bottom of the door, where the concierge slips the mail and magazines through.

Reduce his movements to a minimum, so as to avoid the sound of metallic scrapings that accompany the dragging of the ball on the ground.

Don't speak any more, don't breathe anymore, if possible.

His bed is a refuge when he's under the sheets and blankets—but provided he not fall asleep: the ball might slowly roll with the rhythm of a fitful sleep and end up falling onto the floor with a horrible commotion.

And after that abrupt waking, no more sleep possible.

He awaits dawn with the stress of the alarm clock that rings, of the telephone that puts its two cents in, and of those people who are knocking at his door.

Simon Bièvre freed himself from the ball chained to his ankle. Or perhaps he thought he did?

As for the magistrate who did not really understand what the accused was supposed to have done, he is forced to defend himself vigorously so he will not be condemned in his place.

Contre-courant

In the courtroom, after the usual questions to establish identity, the magistrate calls back the prosecutors. To the accused: "You are accused of naïveté, of questionable charity, and of a selfless act." The facts are there: during the night of May 17 of the preceding year, a neighbor whom the accused did not know knocked on his door and asked him to lend him some money. The defendant, after some hesitation, which constitutes aggravating circumstances, because there is premeditation, finally lent five thousand francs to his neighbor, without interest, and without having him sign a note!

Indignation from the jury.

His fiancée is really worried about the outcome of the trial.

And she is right. The next day the trial turns into a tragedy. The defendant is heard by the court. But he certainly behaves as if he, himself, wanted to lose. Polite, gentle, honest, responding as best he can to the questions of the magistrate. The jury goes crazy: they are personally offended by this monster of generosity. The magistrate reacts: a little indulgence, for heaven's sake! He decides to clear the courtroom. But there is general consternation: how can a magistrate speak like that? What will become of us if the magistrates act like the accused? (. . .)

In the next part: the fiancée is then accused by the magistrate: she loves the accused. She truly loves him. Isn't that as serious as charity or indulgence?

The fiancée defends herself strongly: her intended earns twenty-eight thousand francs a month, which explains her eagerness to defend him. The crowd is calmed by this news.

The character who was dreaming that he was accused cries out in his bed. He wakes up. His girlfriend comes into the room and asks him what's wrong. He answers that he was having a nightmare. At breakfast she asks him for some money, since she's out. Not to mention that it would be high time to ask his neighbor to pay back the

five thousand francs he owes. "How could you have been such a
sucker to lend it to him?"

What is very interesting in this text is the relationship maintained between the dream and reality. Indeed, in the fiancée's
attitude there is something infinitely more icy than in the hyster-
ical outbursts in the courtroom, which would tend to make us
see in the nightmare not an inversion of reality, but rather a
euphemization of it.

A certain number of bureaucrats who are overburdened,
overwhelmed, or prevented from carrying out their jobs attempt
to overcome their condition by adhering to a strict observance
of the rules. From the satirical works of playwright Georges
Courteline (1858–1929) we well know what kind of aberration
this type of strategy can lead to. We are therefore not too surprised to see a subway conductor sentence a couple who have
lost their tickets to spend the rest of their lives underground
(*Voyage à l'ombre*); or a Société Nationale des Chemins de Fer
agent issue a citation to two Siamese twin sisters who had only
bought one ticket (*Le royaume du Siam*); or a meter maid,
called a *Smurfette*—undoubtedly because of her blue clothes—
issuing tickets without rhyme or reason. With the removal of
national borders, with European unity, things can assume an
unprecedented size. One then finds oneself faced with a much
more highly advanced administration, one endowed with a very
efficient machinery, on the scale of its ambitions: the most powerful computers have advantageously replaced the archaic type-
writers of the shabby government offices. The results, however,
are scarcely more reassuring.

Le flux et le refus

To ease the traffic jams of the past years and to preserve
energy, the members of the European Community produced a new regulation to designate the vacation spots for
each of the member countries. Standing on a platform in

front of the television cameras, an announcer provides a simulation: he randomly points out the participants who approach him with a delighted air, and leave more or less happily, depending on the destination they have drawn. After each drawing an arrow is placed on a map of Europe. The results are as follows: the French are to go to Belgium, the Belgians to Switzerland, it being understood that the number of French in Belgium will have to correspond to the number of Belgians in Switzerland. As for the Swiss, they will go to Italy, and so forth. The map lights up with a series of arrows indicating the obligatory migratory flow. For trips within France, Parisians will find out their destinations by drawing lots as they go through tollbooths. [One can easily imagine the complications that will result from these attempts at orchestration. But the moral of the story is its epilogue, with a return to chance, which says a lot about the limits of technocratic rationalization:] At sunset, in a fabulous office whose bay windows overlook the city, a bureaucrat closes a file entitled "Project to harmonize the leisure time of Europeans." He ponders for a moment . . . then takes a lottery ticket from his briefcase and begins to choose his numbers.

If the circle of administrative interventions is widened and reaches international dimensions, not only do the risks of bureaucratic derailment or technocratic overkill multiply, but the slightest relative error assumes cataclysmic proportions.

Que fait-on des restes?

The Director's Office of the Receptions and Banquets Department (or DORBD) made an enormous blunder while preparing for the United Nations international conference on malnutrition. An unfortunate typographical error confused the number representing thousands of tons of butter intended for the Third World with the number of participants in the above-mentioned conference. This is why a banquet for 5,876 people was ordered, paid for, and delivered, whereas the various delegations represented only 327 place settings. It is therefore essential to make these monstrous stocks of food and drink discretely disappear. A phoney import-export company is assigned the task: the cases are to be loaded onto a boat and dumped at sea. [The story ends in the port of Fécamp, where the crates, distributed by mistake, end up with the local fishermen who are delighted by their contents of champagne, paté, coq au vin and chocolate truffles, exhibited before an astonished crowd. Here and there, on the jetty, on the decks of fishing boats, on the rocks, sumptuous feasts break out.]

All of this indeed shows how far we have come from the Althusserian representations of the seventies. Institutions no longer have anything in common with an ideological state apparatus. They are neither driving belts, or relays. They do not assure the permanence of oppression. Nor are we living in a Foucauldian representation of a widespread disciplinarian power that aims to assure the total control of the individual. In fact, institutions no longer have any power at all. They are overwhelmed, incompetent, and surpassed by the size of their task. This is why they are no longer capable of ensuring the viability of a social order. Critical and revolutionary positions were buttressed against a highly structured society that they hoped to overthrow in order to reestablish a more just order. But what to do if this same society simply came apart at the seams?

In the synopses we sense a disquiet concerning these developments, for the failure of instituted regulations has opened the door to the law of the strongest. It opens the door, without any means to close it, to the absolute cynicism of uncontrolled individuals. It is with this in mind that the presentation of the darkest characters of the collection can begin.

THE HUNGER OF DEVELOPERS

The darkest figure we encounter is that of the real estate developer. He appears in many of the texts as a completely caricatural personage. In a certain sense it might be said that within himself he has concentrated all the negative elements that in other times served to create the image of the exploitative bourgeoisie who were solely motivated by a quest for profit. In a universe where the rich are in any case not very likable, the developer is distinguished from his peers by the fact that he has maintained a direct hold on the world that surrounds him: whereas the others have lost control of the instruments of global domination and seek simply to hang on individually to what power and money they have left in a world that is beyond their control, the developer is still the master of all worldly mechanics and workings: he decides, he expropriates, he constructs, he becomes rich. Straight out of a mythology of the 1970s, he displays the final trappings of capitalist power. He is neither a lowlife nor a degenerate: he's the last of the scoundrels.

Here is the developer in a comedy:

Les Rhododendrons

The next day, strutting on his yacht, a tiger at his feet and rings on his fingers, the shady developer and his accomplice, the mayor of the village, toast the success of their evil-minded plan. At his feet his Indian servant is doing his toenails and talks to him in subtitled Burmese. And he is aided by Sicilian thugs who act discreetly and who ride around in an orange Mustang convertible.

Because of his activities the real estate developer is also the only one to inspire collective actions against him: residents join together to defend their rights and to come up with strategies for resistance: farmers barricade themselves in their farms, the young North Africans of Belleville gather in their squatter's apartments, the retirees gather in their retirement homes. In an imaginary universe where there is no longer any trace of strikes, of social movements, or class struggles, the developer thus succeeds in mobilizing the final remains of organized collective action—which shows more or less imagination in the proposed forms of protest (from a boycott against Christmas gifts among the residents of a retirement home to the conquest of the developer by the amorous young North African woman, including the hand-to-hand combat of the organized farmers)—and is more or less effective in its results (the land is saved in the comedies; lost in all the other texts).

Certain specific objects symbolize the developer's persona as a demiurge better than anything else. These are the scale models with which he surrounds himself. He reduces the world to the dimensions of a plaything.

> The developer, wild with rage, launches into a verbal attack: old people will not dictate to him! Regaining his haughty composure, he unveils with a great sardonic laugh the model of a real estate project, with instead of the rhododendron park—the dock of a marina!

> Or of a cake . . .

La belle vie

> In their luxury trilevel in the Sixteenth Arrondissement, the Lamberts are hosting a business dinner to which local officials are invited, as are Lambert's close collaborators who are working on operation "Belle vie à Belleville." One of Lambert's associates gives a laudatory speech on the operation they are soon to launch. Besides the billions that it will earn the group, the neighborhood, which will bring together the modern, the functional, and the aesthetic, will be a true model for the genre. Everyone applauds, except Lambert, who, having arrived late, seems preoccupied. His wife proudly announces a surprise for the guests. She claps her hands, and immediately two employees enter into the room, rolling a long table on which presides the model for the project. On a small side table, she raises a cloth and unveils the model of the neighborhood in its present condition—made out of cake.

> "Help yourselves!" she says, biting into a building.

Since the developer is completely lacking in scruples, he uses a whole range of ignoble acts to achieve his ends (anony-

mous letters, denunciations, blackmail, false papers, murder);
or more simply, deceptive advertising ("A brochure for the ham-
let of the Fountain of Wisteria. There are no more fountains;
there are no wisteria").

The evil-minded all-powerfulness of the developer is seen
in the variety of his desires: all of France is the object of his
greed—the suburbs, the seashores, the hearts of cities—as is
all that remained of France's charming countrysides. "His building is in fact located right in the middle of a future project,
'village, vacations, clean air,' intended to accommodate a hundred and fifty homes, two supermarkets, a sports center." Somewhere else: "a huge project for a saltwater spa to be built of
concrete"—of concrete, no less. In every instance his involvement translates into the displacement of contented people ("the
Cosmos supermarket was built by forcibly evicting twenty-nine
households who were living happily, by putting seven groceries
out of business, including my father's") and the relocating of
unhappy people.

Le retour d'Hélène Kramp

When her husband dies, a seventy-five-year-old upper-middle-class
woman moves into the millstone house her parents had lived in, on
the edge "of a suburban project from the 1960s–1970s, one of
those inhumane housing projects flowing out of raw concrete, of pre-
fabricated homes, and obscene graffiti": she is going to establish a
private *and free* school there, become friends with the young rappers
("that group of young rapper-wolves with their threatening fangs who
are already excluded enough from the social world"), tame them,
and train them at home, make contact with judges, social workers.
Why is she doing all this? We discover the key to the mystery:
her husband is the famous architect who built those "concrete
mousetraps. Having returned to this area where she had spent her
childhood and youth, and where she had not set foot in forty years,
she understands the human disaster in which the man she had never
ceased to love had participated."

There is no limit to the developer's power, and that power extends over generations, the pinnacle of this extension undoubtedly being reached in a science fiction synopsis that takes place in a housing project at the beginning of the next century. The residents have finally managed to transform their site into a pleasant place to live: children play around the parking lots, a motley population relaxes on deck chairs, fruit trees flower between two concrete blocks. Clotheslines have been strung between two adjoining buildings and clothes whip around as in a Neapolitan sky. But we learn that in fact it is not possible ever to be happy in the suburban projects: this peaceful place is threatened. The residents fight so that their neighborhood will be classified a historical site—against a ruthless ecologist developer who, having sensed the winds of history changing, wants to tear it down and put meadows and fields in its place!

The developer in this story does not act alone; he has a few accomplices. First, there is the mayor of the town, who has allowed himself to be bribed with large quantities of wine and who supports the developer in his undertaking; then a few politicians ("I have greased all the wheels; I only need to turn and they drip oil"); obviously the architect; and eventually the engineer of the Highways Department—who proposes the construction of a large national highway to serve the neighboring cities; it will go through the greenhouse filled with rare plants, flowers, and various trees that Mr. Hervé Coquelin, professor of natural sciences, constructed with his own hands (*Paroles de fleurs*). This evil-minded constellation indicates the authors' wariness with regard to political personnel and elected officials that is manifest primarily on the local level: the entanglement of real estate scandals and the political world. The message gets through easily. But, more generally, this portrayal crystallizes the issues of what is at stake surrounding the problems of space. The developer organizes spatial exclusion within a context in which the place where people live plays an increasingly crucial role in the creation and perpetuating of inequalities. He is therefore in the middle of the chain of responsibilities that places in the same category developers, suburbs, violence, and other elements that are today identified as social problems. That said, the role the developer plays is also related to a more structural phenomenon: the current shifting of struggles in the workplace to struggles related to the environment.[2] The place the developer is given in the synopses and the way in which he is described can only be understood if we note the disappearance of the figure of the boss. The boss can no longer be the enemy since the concern over employment makes it difficult to turn into an adversary a character whose defection is what one fears above all. It is his empty place that the developer occupies. The developer's personality therefore invites an in-depth reading of the problems raised by unemployment. However, if at the summit of the social hierarchy there are no longer any clearly identified class enemies, there are on the other hand a number of noxious individuals who filter throughout society: they are the ones who wield power because they possess a certain specialized knowledge.

THE BETRAYAL OF EXPERTS

Doctors

If according to public opinion doctors have a good, distinguished image, we are forced to note that the same is not true in our synopses. Doctors are frankly not very nice in them: they sometimes make mistakes, think a lot about their careers, quite a bit about money, not too much about their patients. They seek to protect themselves rather than to establish a therapeutic relationship. They practice their profession adequately, that's all. But among them there are three categories of specialists who are judged in a particularly negative way: psychiatrists, plastic surgeons, and organ transplant specialists. Here, the discourse changes: indifferent neutrality gives way to virulent denunciations.

Meanwhile, the traditional figure of the doctor who is attentive to the suffering of his patients, whom he has been following for a long time, is noticeably absent: the family doctor has fallen

2. Michel Wievorka, *La France raciste* (Paris, 1992).

with that image. The physician who has succeeded him in truth no longer incarnates devotion or selflessness. The family doctor has been replaced by more faceless versions: in the suburban housing complexes one hears the screaming sirens of ambulances, one finds oneself holding a number while sitting in emergency room waiting areas. There are no scenes that take place in a doctor's office, which is however, a favorite locale in American soap operas.[3]

La belle vie

It all begins one cold evening in December in a sordid suburb north of Paris. A doctor on night call is summoned for an emergency by a family whose mother has attempted suicide. Paul Quentin parks his emergency vehicle in front of a block of project high-rises and hurries to the designated floor. The elevator doesn't work, and the walls of the stairwell are covered with graffiti. Not wanting to linger in that sinister place, Quentin quickly administers an antidote to the poor woman, and, seeing the husband's difficulty in settling the bill, he leaves without asking for the entire payment.

However, since the illnesses presented are much more often mental rather than physical, the characters of the synopses rely above all on psychiatrists. Which is really not a very good idea when we see the way in which doctors act with their patients: at best, they stupefy them with tranquilizers of all kinds; at worst, they make them dig their own graves, after having diverted their fortune and destroyed their personality. Between the two extremes they use them for experiments that aim to destabilize them, not hesitating to lead them to the brink of suicide to test the validity of their hypotheses (*Professeur Rousseau*). Or they become the accomplices of fickle wives and commit their patients without any justification (*Les spirales de l'inquiétude*), or use hypnosis to make their patients commit crimes

---

3. Robert Allen, *Speaking of Soap Operas* (Chapel Hill, 1985).

they themselves had dreamt of committing with complete im-
punity (*Pour la dernière fois, Jérôme Vasselin a perdu la tête*).

We see the manipulation of souls, but also the manipulation
of appearances: a certain number of cosmetic plastic surgeons,
through their well-known clumsiness, bring about the misfor-
tune of their patients, like the "plastic surgeon in search of absolute beauty," who operates on a woman against her will, leaving
her with a swollen face, covered with stitches that she will hide
forever behind a dark veil. Finally there are surgeons who per-
form the most diverse organ transplants that severely harm their
patients who find themselves with cloned kidneys, used livers,
and chimpanzee hearts. And even worse . . . there is a racist
patient in whom they place the liver of an African who has been
selling himself off in small pieces to buy food (*A vot' bon coeur*).
It is a somber trade. Transplant surgery is related to the idea
of a transfer of identities: with "those pieces of bodies in transit,"[4] to use Ginette Raimbault's expression, much more than
mere pieces of flesh circulate obscurely from one individual to
another.

These three types of cynical and mercenary doctors are similar in that they use the resources of their expertise and their
experience to manipulatory ends. This situation is considered
all the more serious in that those three specialities act upon the
human form or on the very foundations of the personality.

If we now seek to understand why doctors are so ill viewed
we must proceed using analogy and attempt to reveal how their
groups are subdivided. We must first note that when doctors
work within the context of a hospital they are much less Machia-
vellian than when they are in private practice. This should not
be surprising: the reason is that they are working in an institution and are therefore rather overwhelmed. Those in private
practice are highly charged emblematic figures. First, because
they exercise a very well known profession, and a great deal of
social experience is not needed to describe them: they bolster

4. Ginette Raimbault, "Morceaux de corps en transit," *Terrain* 18 (1992).

an easy association. Next, because they have a specific competence based on the possession of an unshared knowledge. But
also because their patients are terribly dependent on them. Finally, because they have a direct relationship with the bodies
of others. If they are grouped with other figures in the world
of the synopses who tend to behave in the same way doctors
do, thus forming a broader category, they may be found among
lawyers and architects, in the specialized professions., as well
as among nurses, teachers, dealers, and pimps, due to their relationship with bodies. But they belong above all with an entire
category of experts: scholars, biologists, geneticists, and a whole
group of scientific researchers. We can then go from the hard
sciences to the social sciences, for psychologists are as pernicious as scholars, then from the possession of a certified knowledge to that of an occult knowledge, by adding on all the
witches, the seers, the fortune-tellers, and people using the evil
powers they possess for personal ends. Twenty-six texts thus fit
into the genre that one might call the glaucous supernatural.
These texts unfold in the category of decomposition and decay,
borrow from the category of metamorphosis, portray a suitable
bestiary (spiders, rats, snakes, toads) and adequate adjectives
(*sticky, viscous*). In this strongly laicized imaginary the noble
and spiritual part of religion is found in reference to art, while
the dark and occult part is absorbed by spiritism and the para-
normal.

Policemen and bureaucrats portray the image of an impo-
tent power. Developers, doctors, scholars, and seers take the
place left vacant by them. All the scenarios tell the same story,
that of the inescapable transformation of knowledge into manipulation: power belongs to the experts, and woe to those who
are excluded!

THE FAILURE OF INTEGRATING VALUES

If social bonds in the world of the synopses are threatened, this
is also because all the people who might be capable of enriching
or preserving them are excluded or marginalized. *We are in fact*

in a universe where the only positive values come from outside the mainstream. Thus no cohesive force can be put in motion. Society is no longer capable of keeping its different members together. It functions, on the contrary, like a gigantic centrifuge that spins a growing fringe element of the population onto the periphery. No text tells the story of their reintegration into the course of ordinary life—or it is told on such a parodic level that it is difficult to know what credence to accord such stories. Indeed, the only characters in the corpus who are presented in a slightly favorable way are, in fact, victims. This does not mean, however, that all marginal characters are presented in a positive light. Many are much too miserable to be the object of such a valorization. The homeless, vagrants, beggars, handicapped, and squatters haunt the synopses while bringing their difficulties of existence into one text and another. Here, too, we are very far from the 1970s representations of marginality: these marginal characters do not have the same flamboyant marginality. They are not the spearheads of a counterculture that provides hope for protest and renewal; on the contrary, they demonstrate a form of resigned weariness that is adapted to the new context of social disorganization along with the dissolution of defined adversaries and the rise of a culture of precariousness. But at the same time we are not in a universe that clearly separates the "ins" and the "outs," to use the terminology of Touraine. Societal borders are not airtight; they are porous—except that the journey is accomplished in only one direction, that of disaffiliation. The marginality in the synopses is irresistibly attractive. It is like a magnet, exercising a magnetic attraction over all the characters. A bit in the same way as the hold of cynicism is not confined to the summit of the social hierarchy, but is diffused into the entire social body, just as the culture of marginality is not limited to characters who accept it, but is in fact widely disseminated. And all those who might preserve the social bond are rejected beyond the course of normal everyday life.

Immigrants

The immigrant serves as an exemplary figure of the excluded. In fact, immigrants appear often in the scenarios and always in difficult situations: all the texts concerned tell the story of a failed immigration, and never a success story.

We can distinguish two types of stories in the synopses. The first, often autobiographical, seeks to describe the struggles of an immigrant in a realistic way: the authors evoke the wrenching away at the departure, the difficulty of finding work, the harshness of winter, and the impossibility of integration. Quite often the text ends with the tale of a return to the native land. The second type has a much more ideological aim: it is a militant undertaking that aims to deliver an antiracist message. The authors seek to make their convictions known. Of all the subjects broached in the material, this is the only one around which authors are truly mobilized: undoubtedly because they believe that racism is the most burning problem of society. Immigrants are the last cause.

Some of these texts appear as the author's testimony, which is often explained in the very detailed explanatory notes that accompany them. The authors readily state the personal nature of their story: "The reasoning we all share, when the decision to leave becomes irreversible, is 'I'm going. I'll make a small fortune, then I'll come back'" (*Le départ*). And the author of *Retour des palombes* specifies: "This story is the story of my life and of that of a good number of our African brothers. Any resemblance to real people is far from coincidental." The note of intent sometimes takes the form of a true dissertation: "The reasons why one leaves one's country are many, but can be summed up by two elements: one economic and the other political, or both at the same time" (*Fortuné*). It may describe a militant act: "When immigration and particularly clandestine immigration is at the center of the debate in French political parties, it is imperative that a film on this subject be made by an African. In the collective unconscious of the communities called 'host,' clandestine immigrants are perceived as a seething and threatening mass of depersonalized, even dehumanized, individuals; it is imperative within the current context to make their stories, their hopes, the reasons that push them onto the difficult path of immigration reappear, to give them back shape, soul, and life."

First-generation immigrants are presented as victims of the

period of industrial euphoria: they hold menial jobs, difficult and dangerous trades, earn low salaries, are exploited at work, have unhealthy living conditions. They speak the host language poorly, cannot make themselves understood, live in isolation and exclusion. They might suffer job-related illnesses, as does Sory, who was probably exposed to radiation during the time when he worked in a company that handled industrial cleaning, who goes back to his own country to die of cancer: "The palm wine having gone slightly to his head, Sory begins to speak in an exalted way: 'They really fooled us, us immigrants, in the land of the Whites. We would have done better to stay in our own country. There were so many things to do here. Why do we wear ourselves out plowing fields in the land of the Whites when our own land is drying up for lack of nourishment by the sweat of Africans'" (*Le retour des palombes*).

The hostility that immigrants encounter prevents any hope for their integration: social exclusion is reinforced by geographical exclusion. Exposed to multiple adversities, they cannot, for example, acquire their own lodging. The theme of the unobtainable house is developed, for example, in *La lézarde:*

Oufkir Samara has just won the grand prize in the lottery drawing organized by the directors of the Batimou company—the giant in the building industry. Having recently arrived in France, he is unknown by those who work there; they seek him out and finally find him in a lodging in the suburbs. They take him to an elegant building where a very high-class cocktail party awaits him. He is solemnly given the keys to his new home. He is the hero of the hour. Late that night he is driven to an isolated little house, the one that he has really won: it is covered with cracks. A mysterious concrete-eating plant is the cause of the deterioration. Oufkir untiringly attempts to plug up the cracks, but in vain: as soon as an opening is filled, another opens up. The little house patched up in this way is metamorphosed by these successive additions, but the plant, unkillable, ends up taking over. There is a strong ecologist organization (Guérilla Verte), a militant lover, the glare of the media spotlight; multiple vicissitudes that feed this story that the author describes as "social realism seeped in the bizarre."

Immigrants are also refused another means of integration: integration through marriage. The host country offers neither its land nor its women. Eight projects portray mixed couples and the difficulty they have staying in love. One author describes "the modern and true story of a love crushed by the incomprehension of cultures." In one text a young Algerian woman tells of her brothers' violent reservations upon hearing of her engagement to a young French man. In another, it is the opposite situation that is the source of distress.

Nous étions trois

(*This scene occurs the day Julia decides to introduce Amine, the young student with whom she is in love and whom she has decided to marry, to her family, who belong to the middle-class bourgeoisie.*)

MADAME BENOÎT: Who would like more potatoes?
MONSIEUR BENOÎT: Say, Amibe . . . Are you really Kabyle?
JULIA (cutting him off): Papa . . . It's *Amine.*
MONSIEUR BENOÎT: Yes, of course, sorry! Uh . . . Habib!
. . . Aaah!. . . I'll never get it!
MARIE: No, Papa! A-M-I-N-E.
MONSIEUR BENOÎT: Excuse me, I'm inexcusable! . . . I have to get used to it. Yes . . . what was I saying . . . You are Kabyle.

Failures at integration often result in a return to the native land, as is explained by an Antillean author in his note of intent: "without having exact figures, we can estimate the number of those who wish to return home at 95 percent." Whether it is possible, impossible, real or virtual, unfortunate or even fortunate as in *Revoir Balombé,* returning home appears to be the only way to escape present difficulties. It is this repeated message that enables us to understand the full meaning of the French experience that, in the end, is a journey of disappointment. We should note that three-quarters of the texts devoted to first-generation immigrants are written by authors who were themselves born abroad.

The texts devoted to young second-generation immigrants have a rather different tone. We leave the universe of work and exploitation to enter into that of the suburbs, of forced idleness, and of violence. The protagonists remain victims, but not in the same way: assigning them that role assumes the development of a rhetoric that broadly imputes responsibility to the entire social context. The authors attempt to protest against racial hatred: "*Ratonnade* is a film that denounces the violence of certain young people who want to exclude from their environment other young people with obvious ethnic differences, seizing the first pretext they find to enflame the hatred of the other that they carry inside them." The conclusion is also accompanied by a moral that is either implicit or explicit, but always clear. It is thus that we see a hunted-down foreigner perish with his entire family at the end of a manhunt. The man was a scholar who had just made a scientific discovery of great importance, which would have enabled a huge improvement in the conditions of human life (*L'espoir manqué*). In another text, a fortunate occurrence ends up uniting two feuding families who live on the same floor of the same public-housing building in the same housing project: little ten-year-old Karim is stricken with a serious illness, and his blood type is extremely rare. But Luc, the young white racist, has the same blood type. He agrees to the transfusion. Everyone is gathered together at Karim's hospital bedside, and Karim is cured while mixed blood is coursing through his veins. A highly symbolic metaphor, since the exchange of blood enables a form of ritual fraternity (*Les deux soleils*).

Authors also evoke the problem of violence. The theme is not avoided, rather it is dealt with head-on: the authors do not attempt to broach the question of immigration from another angle. We don't see any little *beurs* (French children of North African origin) at school or in summer camp, we don't see any at work or in the military. They are in the projects, they wander, they tag, they rap, they watch. By proceeding in this way the authors confirm de facto the connection between immigration and delinquency, which is established in the stereotypes of the ideology they are fighting against. But, starting from there, they attempt to replace that connection within its context, to explain it, to justify it, to relativize it.

First they must show that this violence is not innate: it is a response to aggression that comes from elsewhere, in the form of verbal attacks and insults, but also in the form of physical violence: chasing, hunting down, manhunts. The synopses detail the attacks of which the young foreigners are the object: we find that in the unfolding of violence, they are never the first to act. They attempt at all costs to avoid battle, by seeking paths for negotiation. ("Nouri tries to get away. The boys reach him and hold him against a wall.") When they are forced to defend themselves to save their lives or their honor, they do so unwillingly ("Amar has to hit Baptiste, whereas he would have preferred to make him a friend, a brother," *Dernier round*). Sometimes it is a matter of pure simulation, like the story of the young man who, in order to be accepted by the parents of the girl he loves, asks his gang to stage a mugging: by intervening as a savior, he wins both the respect of the parents and the heart of the maiden. Other synopses place the emphasis on the conditions in which young immigrants live: violence is no longer a simple reply to an isolated act of aggression, it is a form of response to the social and geographical exclusion that weighs on them. It is within this context that we meet the young heroic *beur* who will reestablish order, fight against the drug dealers, and save the projects in crisis. In fact, he doesn't exactly have the qualities of a Hollywood hero: he is rather cunning, nice, somewhat wily, not always completely courageous. Like Karim, who is forced to assume the role of leader of his gang when it is faced with the death of its leader, who overdosed: he decides to seek justice and carries out a parallel investigation into the drug network that is supplying his project. Or like Rachid, cofounder with his girlfriend Isabelle of the organization SOS Cultural Friendship, who works with the mayor in an attempt to resolve the problems of the Montillet projects:

La vie en HLM

Hello, Mr. Mayor. I am proud to speak on behalf of my friends, to tell you . . . uh . . . that we want to form an organization. Well, I wanted to tell you that for our organization . . . we will need a room as soon as possible where we can do photography, music, get together, since we always have to hold our meetings in the stairwell of the building.

Or finally, like Aziz who helps Blanche deliver her little girl from the hell of drugs and the clutches of her pimp:

Sortie blanche

Aziz, a young nineteen-year-old Moroccan, lives in hiding in Barbès. He left Morocco and settled in France without the proper papers. Living by petty schemes, he fell under the influence of a pimp who used him to sell drugs and find girls. He is "extremely self-sufficient, smart, a braggart, a charmer." The ties that connect him to an old lady who has shown him the kindness that has been lacking since his arrival in France cause him to experience a true awareness of the misery of his life: "While standing up to the pimp he knows he is risking losing everything, being sent to prison or being sent back to Morocco, but at the same time he will rid himself of his delinquent values."

Aziz's redemption is a rather unusual case. Much more often the stories end badly.

Rap Side Story

A brilliant inspector, who has recently been promoted, asks, to everyone's surprise, to be stationed in the headquarters of a dangerous suburb. Last summer, during a wave of violence, youths destroyed the shopping center. Ever since those incidents the police no longer dare to hazard into the projects. Two gangs fill the pages of the newspapers with their reciprocal animosity. The first gang is made up of French, the second of immigrants or sons of immigrants. "He notices that the accumulated hatred has generated a formidable energy that is simmering. But how to harness it?" During his patrols, "he is very impressed by the rap music that he hears on every street corner and whose heavy basses accompany a flow of threatening words that seem to spread like wildfire." The laxity and the cynicism of the police who work around him are very depressing. One evening, when he gets home, he grabs the remote control "perhaps finally to zap himself" and happens on *West Side Story*. He then comes up with the idea of staging a rap musical with the two gangs, where each would describe its dreams, its specific hells. It will be called *Rap Side Story*. The project begins well, but racial hatred ultimately wins out.

All of these synopses follow the rules of interpretation and demystification: the authors' words find support in racist discourse, sometimes purely and simply to overthrow it through a sort of symbolic joke, and sometimes to emphasize its virulence, sometimes to replace it in its context. Always to relativize it. Everything occurs as if the authors were indexing the arguments of common racism and were refuting them one after the other. It is a perfectly organized discourse of response that has made the issue of violence the center of its focus. This is the only subject in the material about which the authors defend a biased point of view, as if it were the only cause that to them truly appears to justify a mobilization. But at the same time, in these scripts the story of immigration, with its hopes, its dreams, and its myths, is ultimately destroyed.

THE YEARNING FOR INTERPERSONAL VALUES

The Elderly

Added to the classic image of the excluded immigrant we find other, less conventional figures who are unique in their nature and their characteristics. Foremost among them are the elderly. They might be likely to maintain interpersonal bonds. They are in fact clearly invested with positive values, and the entire meaning of their involvement here is built around their interpersonal competence. They inspire unanimous sympathy, generally fed on shared experience and complicity, much more rarely on compassion: enthusiastic, upbeat, and warm characters, the elderly adore life, are generous and active, understanding and industrious. They have inspired primarily comedies in which they are kind and good-hearted actors. But when they appear in psychological dramas or in romantic comedies, their image, less forced, is not fundamentally different: they exhibit the same impartiality, the same openness to adventures and encounters, that mixture of a love for others and a love of life that allows them to escape the general interpersonal chaos endured and maintained by the generations that have followed them.[5] They are, however, bearers of an ambiguous message since we don't really know whether the talents they are recognized to have are the result of their age or of their generation. In other words, is it the accumulation of experience that gives them their interpersonal competence, or is it because in their time people still had recipes for friendship?

The synopses first emphasize their physical abilities: "alert" and "lively," they "good-humoredly" live what remains of their lives. Not hesitating to climb mountains, to take part in a car chase, or to do a headstand—their feet against the wall and their head on the ground—even, if fate forces them into it, to throw a troublesome "bully" to the carpet with an aikido hold or a simple leg-trip. This is a deliberately optimistic vision of the aging process that spares the body and the mind any deterioration. For psychological health goes hand in hand with physical vitality: full of vigor and vivacity, they "burst out laughing, are all excited, have a great time," while at the same time they escape any form of standardization: "An eccentric old lady, an extravagant old man. An original."

5. The fact that elderly people appear primarily in comedies leads us to question the meanings that the authors wanted to convey through their characters. Do these texts translate an obsession with the aging of the population by using comedic devices to recycle a latent concern—or do they instead speak of the joyful improvement in the physical conditions of elderly people that happens to coincide with the reappearance of "the new third age" that combines physical health, the improvement of financial resources, and availability? In any case, it is certain that in texts that are not comedies the story that is then generally told is that of an unusual friendship between an elderly person and another very different character, with whom the older person had absolutely no a priori reason to get along. In other words, elderly people have the same type of profile in more serious texts. They are a bit more weary than in the comedies, a little less immortal, but their essential quality—their ability to love—remains the same.

What they have gained in dynamism they have lost in wisdom: the old man is no longer the ancestor whose eyes are full of light, and his accumulated experiences have not taught him reason. Except, of course, in works of historical fiction or perhaps, then, very far from the city, in the countryside: in those archaic villages deep in the woods there still remain a certain number of witches who know the secret of the plants and call the birds by their names. However, in an amnesiac society in which all knowledge is so quickly stricken with obsolescence, it is not accumulated knowledge that confers their superiority upon the elderly. Their expertise is elsewhere: it is, it would seem, above all in their ability to live intense relationships.

One can, in fact, wonder whether among all the qualities that are recognized in the elderly, the primary one is not that extraordinary interpersonal ability: they are capable of having relationships with the most diverse people. They are attached to children, live great stories of love, and above all, in the heart of the retirement homes, nursing homes, or "death houses" in which they have been placed (abandoned? locked up?) they are likely to have more structured ties with their peers: they organize red-hot poker games, go arm in arm to the racetrack at Deauville, when they're not going off on a trip to the Caribbean. They circulate without the slightest difficulty from the top to the bottom of the social hierarchy, from the inside to the outside of the boundaries of morality, traverse ages, generations: they are paragons of sociability.

It is very interesting that these qualities are honored in this way: we are quite far here from the virile virtues of the Hollywood hero, from the moral dilemma of the romantic hero, or from a confrontation with fate as experienced by characters in ancient tragedies—in our synopses what makes the stuff of a hero is not an act of courage or of sacrifice; it is the ability to break down the barriers of solitude.

There are only three cases of bad-tempered and ill-willed old ladies. And in each of these cases the point of view reported is that of an employee responsible for taking care of the person, as if the fact that the woman occupies a hierarchical position is enough to render her disagreeable. On the other hand, when a character has the good fortune to be both old and a (petty) thief, his positive characteristics are potentialized to the point of raising him to the heights of charm and seductiveness.

Les papys flingueurs

Louis and André are residents of a retirement home, Les Marronniers, located in a Paris suburb. Louis always appears polite, elegant, a bit of old France. André is more natural. To hear them talk, their past was rather troubled. They were more or less involved in business, lived the high life, before suffering a reversal of fortune that led them to Les Marronniers.

In truth, they are two former petty thieves who have spent their lives dreaming of "the big deal" that would make them rich, without ever being able to obtain it. (. . .) They are particularly well liked by the director, who finds them charming and always cheerful. What she doesn't know is that they pay their bills with their winnings from the track, with the complicity of old pals from the racetracks, and even with the help of the three-card trick, where their age really comes in handy in duping their victims. Nor does she know that in the home they break regulations by organizing nocturnal poker games, invite girlfriends of somewhat dubious morality during afternoon dances. Their escapades have, moreover, a salubrious effect on the morale of the other retirees.

Elderly people also live beautiful, often very romantic, love stories with charming preliminaries—bouquets of flowers, boxes of candy, compliments and blushing. Sometimes they are less platonic, as for Louisa, "an eternal lover always ready to be set on fire," or Mildred, a former cabaret dancer, charming under her red wig, who leads the calm existence of a little old retired woman. "Her only slipups are sentimental: every pair of pants makes her heart beat; every six months, disappointed, she empties a bottle of scotch. And every other time the police take her to the hospital. When she comes out she celebrates her freedom with her roommates" (*Pas de mouron dans les mouroirs*).

Elderly people have intense social relationships: first, because they have been living for a long time, they have accumulated a considerable number of friendships, which they can renew any time the opportunity presents itself. This is the case, for example, of Colette and Mildred: "Colette, a tall beanpole who has seen seventy-eight springs, has not always been on the streets. When, in Room 106 of the hospital where she seeks refuge, sort of like when one goes to a hotel, she finds her friend Mildred, little Mildred whom she used to protect in high school, she is wild with joy. Together, in the enthusiasm of their reunion, they will make many plans." Then, since the elderly know the price of friendship, they also know how to organize its forms: regular outings, group travel, cruises, good meals, card games— with a strong predilection for the poker-dance-party where couples in love embrace each other tenderly to the sound of violins. They go to the movies together, to sporting events or boxing matches, and their commentaries are not lacking. In other words, they do not hesitate to anchor a relationship in the long term, to accept structured forms, and at the same time they are capable of that mixture of concessions and solidarity integral to life within a group.

Their attachment to relationships is pivotal: all of their behavior may be analyzed through that prism. Indeed, two types of plots feed the synopses: in the first, the retirees organize themselves to save their residences, which bear names of flowers ("les Rhododendrons," "les Bleuets," "les Lilas"), from the clutches of real estate developers; in the second type they (again) organize themselves to escape from the prisonlike environment of the rest homes, retirement homes, asylums, or death houses in which they are sequestered. But the same inspiration lies behind these two different types of attempts: to carry on an impeded interpersonal adventure in the best conditions possible. The ends justify the means: emptying the safes of the

shady developer to blackmail him; fomenting a mutiny to reno-
vate the buildings and ease the regulations (*Après la vie, la vie,
ou le cimetière des éléphants*); organizing discrete breakouts
that go unnoticed; or preparing a true escape: *Les mutins de
l'Arche,* true to their biblical metaphor, will flee onto a barge
during a flood, while at the same time freeing the antelopes and
the iguanas from the neighboring zoo.

A more general precept is hidden behind the figure of the
elderly person: the only people capable of promoting a little
humanity are located in the margins of social life. From this
point of view the elderly and children are in the same category.
It is, moreover, undoubtedly the reason why they get along so
well. Indeed, the elderly have once again assumed a certain
number of characteristics traditionally attributed to children:
this is why they are called "wild," and "incorrigible"—in an age
when we almost never dream of correcting children—they play
pranks and tricks, they enjoy secrets and hiding things, tell tall
tales while giving free rein to their overflowing imagination
("He tells his incredible adventures to whoever wants to listen,
from the time when he was a pirate and a smuggler and a cap-
tain and engaged to an Arab princess"). But often their young
companions seem infinitely more reasonable than they do: they
remind them that they have to go to school or that they have
little chance of finding the lost stripes of Arthur's pajamas. It
is as if permutation of good sense and reason had occurred between the two extremities of life.[6]

Les mutins de l'Arche

(The scene takes place in the common room of the Ark, where Madame Carrington is handing out the words to the song that she wants
the retirees to practice. But the latter are going to give her quite a
few problems . . .)

---

6. There are nevertheless a dozen texts that have a rather different tone, in fact;
they do not mention children, but rather childhood. And childhood is then associated
with the marvelous. We find some common accessories (marionettes, fans, hand
puppets, dolls—often broken) and a few favored interlocutors (fairies, elves, Santa
Clauses, clowns).

Madame Carrington (in a high-pitched voice): "Today, as I told some of you yesterday, we are going to learn a song which I'm sure will put you in a good mood. It is called 'J-O-Y,' which spells *joy*. Ha, ha, ha! (*To Norbert*) Norbert, my little Norbert, would you like to pass these words out to your little friends? That's wonderful. While Norbert is passing them out I am going to sing the melody for you once. Then it will be your turn. One, two, three . . .

(*Norbert eagerly does his job.*)

Madame Carrington (singing in a very shrill voice):
J-O-Y, J-O-Y, joy, joy, joy
Our law is good cheer and joy, joy, joy
We cannot do without joy, joy, joy,
J-O-Y, J-O-Y, joy, joy, joy!

(But when she asks the residents to repeat in chorus, they let out a shrill scream, then sing out all together "Le curé de Camaret," "L'Internationale," "La Madelon," and other rowdy drinking songs, in the most outrageous cacophony.)

Racket in the dining hall, clandestine meetings, and organized riots are much more evocative of the classrooms of the Third Republic than the anomic brouhaha that undermines teachers today. "Louis and André organize a secret meeting with some other retirees, among them Agathe and Alice, two sisters who are somewhat in love with the two robbers. Each participant proposes a solution: petition, boycott of Christmas presents, a sit-in, but the meeting ends in chaos" (*Les papys flingueurs*).

In fact, one might wonder whether the inversion is not in part linked to the change of status of some of those involved. With the increase in life expectancy and the evolution of the way aging is dealt with, there are now more elderly people in such establishments. It is therefore not surprising that comedies endow them with strategies of resistance usually attributed to schoolchildren. Inversely, the transformation of models of education has caused children to earn a new autonomy.

Children

Children take advantage of that situation at every opportunity: in a group, kids from catechism class will snatch the main character in *Bébé-cloche* from the horrors of the Direction Départementale de l'Action Sanitaire et Sociale; those from natural science class will save their professor from the clutches of the police (*Paroles de fleurs*); those from the elementary grades will stop a runaway train. One little girl will uncover the con artists who tricked the "lucky" winners of bogus televised games (*Les lubies de Lola*). Another will give shelter to an ailing panhandler.

Children's achievements are such that they are able to lead very independent lives, which ultimately suits their parents very well. In fact, we see a whole series of texts focusing on the mastery children have acquired in the realm of computer science. The extreme dexterity with which they can press the buttons on the controls of video games serves as a fulcrum for the development of a new conception of childhood. That conception advances children's very specific and completely exclusive abilities (parents are not associated with them): children are capable of stopping a runaway computer, of changing a program from a distance, of hacking into data banks, of deciphering obscure codes, of connecting scattered information. This brings a new portrait of childhood into focus, one that onto traditional human qualities (enthusiasm, freshness, imagination, mischievousness, that entire constellation of virtues that are tied to the age) adds intellectual qualities connected to the mastery of modern technologies: penetrating intelligence, quickness, mobility, wisdom.

Their precocious introduction to life issues gives them an affective maturity that enables them to lavish their own parents with the judicious advice that adults so greatly need in order to manage their troubled romantic and sexual lives. All of this gives a rather paradoxical result: entire synopses vibrate with the consequences of new uncertainties and new disorders. The world in which the characters evolve has become so complicated since it is no longer organized and simplified by global systems of interpretation; for adults anxiety becomes the price of deliverance; but children miraculously possess the keys to the world's complexity. They save a couple's relationship, restore friendship to their parents, return to adults their taste for life. Children are neither naive, nor malleable, they are not the ones whom one teaches; they are the ones who already know. They understand everything!

The Innocents

Children and the elderly are the concrete embodiments of a more general notion: that a true bond can be established only by distancing oneself to a certain degree from the rules of the social game. Some characters who have been miraculously saved, strong figures in every instance, also join these emblematic figures.

Histoire d'Amour

This screenplay recounts "the vicissitudes of a young man with a tender heart who is thrown into a world without innocents." The form chosen combines the documentary with journalism: the off-camera voice of a journalist sums up the edifying stages in the life of Love: his birth ("from a mother officiating over her paved territory of the rue Saint Denis" and an unknown father), his abandonment to the DDASS, his placement in an adoptive family with other children from the four corners of the world. We can already perceive his sense of justice and his taste for great causes ("Love intervenes between a little Chinese girl and a little black boy who are fighting about who will have a doll. Love takes the doll, gives the head to the girl and the rest of the body to the boy. The two unhappy children throw the pieces in his face"), his peaceful education ("the disciplines in which he excels are sports and raffles"), his courageous undertakings ("One day at school Love is the victim of severe reprisals from all the boys who attack him for having defended a little girl in a jump rope dispute. Today, Madame Dupuis, the directress of the school, remembers . . ."). He is then a victim of a fight that he wanted to prevent and ends up in prison for a crime he didn't commit. Freed at the end of five years for good behavior, he decides to establish an association for the down-and-out and the poor. After attempting unsuccessfully to prevent a boxing match by coming between the two opponents, Love is involved in a bus accident that kills sixty-six people. He is the only survivor. Suddenly, he is given a television show. He would like very much to use it to collect funds for his association. The show is a ratings triumph. "The market is immediately inundated with T-shirts and pins portraying the image of the new missionary of peace." The show then becomes a series: Love finds himself in front of an enthralled audience while the host implores them to recognize his immense goodness. At the switchboard the questions pour in; a viewer even asks him the winning lottery number. Love refuses everything at first, but pushed by the host gives six numbers at random. He unfortunately does not have time to talk about his association, for he has to give up the microphone. At the end of the show, there is excitement in households: the state lottery records a level of participation that had never before been reached, but the numbers Love gave do not come out . . . this time. They are picked a few days later. "It is a triumph for Love. Now he is invited to participate in television game shows to bring luck to teams, and by employers, as the working class requests him to rule on conflicts."

It is then that Love meets Melanie, with whom he falls—"without admitting anything"—madly in love. She indeed senses that they are exploiting his naïveté and would like to protect him, but she can't. In the end Love moves in with her in the suburbs of Paris: they adopt children from all over the world and continue to receive all the outcasts of modern life.

The enormous feedback Love receives from public opinion, the interest he inspires in the media, are clearly expressed in the dialogued scene:

Public comment (sidewalk interviews of February 18, 2010, between 10:00 A.M. and 8:00 P.M.)

QUESTION: What do you think of Love?
A WOMAN: Listen, I think he is a completely obliging boy,

especially since he had a difficult childhood, I believe. No, he seems quite nice.

A YOUNG MAN: Love? He's a guy . . . a complete innovator. He has completely understood what people are lacking: some sort of goodness. You know what I mean? He reminds me of that sentence of Malraux's: "The Twenty-First century will be religious or it won't be." That's it in a nutshell. But you know, people won't understand it until afterward.

A GENTLEMAN: What gets me is the media. He's just like the others, he'll be taken over by the media. It's true; I'm sick of it. One day it's China, the next day it's Hungary. In the meantime it's always the citizen who has to pay for political stupidity.

A TEENAGE GIRL: I like him a lot. Because in the end he's true. But I get the feeling that people are taking advantage of him.

A LADY: I don't trust that kind of individual: an ex-con reconverted into show business. And then, first of all, why does he call himself "Love"?

A GENTLEMAN: What do I think of Love? (*Laughs*) I have the feeling he fits in perfectly in our time. People need to attach themselves to symbols, so why not generosity? And it's better than violence.

A GENTLEMAN: If I were him I would win the lottery and take off for the Antilles or somewhere else.

SHE: We watch him all the time on TV. I think he has courage, and then he believes in it, that's important.

A TEENAGE BOY: He's a great guy. He's against war and injustice. Love is the savior of the poor.

A GENTLEMAN: Guys who are lucky like that—there's one in a century.

A LADY: Ultimately people are pitiful. All that interests them is money. Love is a trap.

AN OLD MAN: What do I think of him?.A lot of good . . . love is a great and beautiful thing, my friend. Here, take for example that boy who's on TV. We should all be like

him. Just imagine, my friend . . . that would be something
else again, don't you think?

Poor Love, it's true he is great! We can certainly see why
the media are involved. We can certainly understand why they
turn him into a model, a star, an arbiter, that his photo, his
image, his merchandise are in great demand. But we must also
recognize that in the meantime intelligence suffers a great blow
from all this. But it is not very surprising: it is only because Love
is a little bit stupid that he can be generous. It is because he
has not understood the rules of the social game that he can
break them. And this is not all; in addition, luck has to play a
part. This fact explains his privileged connections to the lottery,
to chance, and to destiny throughout his life. It is this that makes
him an improbable individual—the only one, right in the middle of the social world, among the ten thousand characters in
the texts, to be the outspoken promoter of justice and generosity. But at the same time he is the perfect mirror image of all
the others and is thus extremely enlightening with regard to
the processes at work in this imagined world. For Love has not
understood—and this is what gives him his strength and what
authorizes his goodness—that he is in a world where cynicism
alone regulates social relationships.

All the same, he does not attempt to convince anyone of
the basic validity of his positions. He does not try to say that
generosity is also a component of human nature, that no social
movement can be explained if it is not understood as a force
driven by the hope for renewal, that purely strategic representations of the social world are not always explanatory, are in any
case partial, and perhaps even inexact since they leave entire
sections of people's motivations and actions in shadow. He does
not seek to reverse the equation and suggest that by chance
it might be cynical people who are the cretins and who have
understood nothing of the functioning of social life. No, he
doesn't put himself on that level: he would certainly be a loser.
The attitude that associates intelligence with suspicion, understanding with distrust, and assimilates generosity with credulity,
is much too solid ever to be changed. This attitude is so wide

reaching that it has enabled the definitive disqualification of opposing notions, reducing them to the traditional positions of those who have ostensibly not yet understood the truth of human nature, or worse, of people who are even more cynical than others since they have incorporated the gamut of good intentions into their manipulatory plans. This is a shame. The author thus leaves Love to accept his limits fully. It is ultimately more reasonable to do so.

THE PROMOTION OF AESTHETIC VALUES

The Infirm

The world of the synopses also makes a lot of room for people who are afflicted with a physical or mental handicap. Characters who are deaf, blind, mute, autistic, polio victims, paralyzed, mentally ill, conjoined sisters, paraplegics, amputees, all lead us into a true *Cour des miracles.*[7] This particular attention that is paid to anomalies contrasts with everyday experience, for modern life seems to be a triumphant procession of healthy bodies that are increasingly homogenized and uniform, due to the progress of medicine, hygiene, and food. Physical appearances have been improved and at the same time made similar, and, with the most seriously handicapped people being relegated to specialized institutions, the imperfect body is increasingly absent from our view.

The same plot often recurs in the synopses: rejected by his parents—especially by his father—after they discover his deformity, the handicapped person, thanks to a fortunate relationship established with someone outside the immediate family (who might be the care giver, a distant uncle, a neighbor, a chance encounter) is able to give free reign to a creativity that will enable him to transform his suffering into a work of art. This is why the texts simultaneously blend the story of a relationship with the story of a creation.

---

7. *Une Cour des miracles* is a negative term for a place inhabited by the downtrodden, the infirm, beggars, and thieves.—TRANS.

A very strong bond is established in a majority of scripts between handicaps and artistic creation. The connection might be made in very different ways, but beyond the various presentations, this intimate relationship between art and an abnormality is continuously reasserted. The person afflicted with a handicap thus might find himself endowed with an innate talent that turns him into a poet: the skewed view he has of the world that surrounds him enables him to establish spontaneous and unexpected relationships between varied images: the person blends the registers of the concrete and the abstract, he arranges raw metaphors in an involuntary and fluid way, leaving the magic of words to act, somewhat the way children do. His particular sensitivity enables him to communicate with natural elements. We then find the underlying, traditional idea that grants the simpleminded a favored relationship with nature, undoubtedly because he cannot master all the rules of his culture. This theme can be expanded to assume modernized versions of the myth of the Good Savage: madness or an infirmity separates one from civilization and draws one nearer to a certain form of natural wildness.

Ils s'appelaient Atlantide

Once upon a time there were some young people in distress, misunderstood, under constant medical scrutiny, spread out in large metropolises bristling with brick and cement buildings. These were the "Mentally Ill." These young people, as the result of a plane crash, wash up onto a deserted and enchanted island in the archipelago of the Azores. They destroy their radio, get rid of their sedatives, and lead a Robinson Crusoe existence at the foot of a volcano, in the midst of smoking geysers, streams of warm water, and flowering trees. "Our characters will decode its lakes, its lava, its shores and its geysers. They will love it as the place where, finally, to live, they were called to appear. Our intention is to show that they were Poets, although they were thought to be crazy."

This theme of the implicit poetry of the simpleminded who speak with words of wisdom is seen again in *L'envol:* a young boy has become mentally handicapped following a motor scooter accident that has put him into a coma lasting several months. A passionate and unexpected relationship is formed between him and his therapist, Catherine, a beautiful, dynamic, and independent young woman. "Mathieu, through his poetic, gentle, and jealous side, will show Catherine her true self. Mathieu, who has become the small, imperfect, handicapped one, will be a mirror for Catherine. He will make her discover her weaknesses, but also her strengths, her true face." The young woman's attachment is due to the emotion evoked by that bizarre language ("Leave it, I am drawing, I am drawing tenderness, my fingers are crayons to paint your heart. The birds are used to write in the sky so that the sky will be free").

In other cases an anomaly does not automatically create talent, but the suffering it has provoked can be reinvested into creation. This is the case of Xavier, for example, whose broken fingers do not keep him from painting:

Comme des fantômes

Xavier is a painter in a group of artists-rockers-actors who stage happenings in abandoned buildings and deserted factories in the suburbs of Paris. He does stenciling in the streets, sketching "the faces of neighborhood people with which he wants to cover the walls of Paris." After they quarrel, the group disbands and Xavier is confronted by a gang of individuals who attack him and crush his hands in the heavy door of an apartment courtyard. All of his fingers are broken. The surgeon who operates on him confirms that he will never be able to hold a pencil again. He meets a young girl, lively and upbeat, who gives him some hope. "The next day he paints—with his hands in casts—an extraordinarily messy figure in front of her home, and scrawls underneath it an almost illegible 'thank you.' Then he leaves Paris." He patiently and tenaciously gets back to work. His inspiration is different now and marked by the trauma he has endured; it is profoundly renewed. He chooses a building that is supposed to be demolished, studies its history, and paints a huge mural that will be destroyed with it. "He paints the portraits of sick people on the walls of an abandoned hospital, profiles of prisoners on a house of detention, portraits of Fassbinder and Kirk Douglas on the front of a German movie house soon to be torn down, the shadows of a group of refugees on the fence of an African immigrant camp, the image of Mayakovski reading a poem on a window of the former headquarters of the Communist Party."

The relationship between the handicapped and art is not necessarily direct: in some synopses the disabled character instead plays the role of mediator, or the one who inspires. This is the case of the young boy with Down's syndrome in *Bois transparents* who enables Alex to find new inspiration and new creative breath. This is also the case of Laurent, who in spite of his passion for music will not become the musician he would have liked to become: following a bout of polio he lives in a wheelchair and tries to learn to play the guitar. He can't do it, but he will inspire the success of his friend (*Laurent et les Sixties*).

The connection between art and a handicap does not involve only the most serious of afflictions. It is found among those who are less gravely stricken: those who are a little too fat, a little too short (*Les journées perdues d'une famille ordinaire*), a little too ignorant (*Irma la naze*). All these characters convey the same message: they have their role to play, their place to be found. Their stigmata are in truth the source of an extraordinary and enriching experience. The theme is enlarged to all forms of marginality.

Pauvre Martin

Martin is too fat. Unkempt, awkward, depressed. With his cumbersome body he encounters only misfortunes: he bumps into the concierge in the too-narrow stairwell, is jostled when he crosses the street, takes up two places when he sits in the subway. He arrives late at the newspaper print shop where he works at night, loses time listening to the tales of his uncharitable colleagues about their amorous conquests, gets himself fired. He goes home, knocks over the cat's bowl, turns on the TV, pretends he is Schwarzenegger. He transfers all his difficulty in living into two packs of cookies, and a butter, chocolate, and pickle sandwich.

Until he answers a casting call: they're looking for a rather corpulent actor to play Falstaff at the Paris theater. "His efforts are conclusive; they hire him. He's a triumph."

In fact, we might question the degree to which this model might represent a double thematic tendency: on the one hand, the tendency toward nonacademic artistic ideology, which encourages belief in a creativity that is no longer connected to the rigor of academic learning but is found entirely in the spontaneous verve of the creative act: art as associated with innocence; powerful creators are empirical, and simple souls have superior clairvoyance. On the other hand, there is the tendency to associate art and religion. The society presented in the material is deeply laicized (we find no allusion to religion in the synopses; there are a few priests, always positive characters—proving they are truly no longer on the side of the powerful—but no indication at all that might suggest any spiritual renewal or a return to the religious). Within this context the artistic experience appears to be substituted for that of the religious: art is the only thing that enables a hero to escape a ponderous everyday existence and to experience a certain form of transcendence. For the handicapped, art enables the conversion of a wounded body into a creative body and gives meaning to their suffering. The loss of physical wholeness is replaced by this new artistic ability. But at the same time, the fact that redemption is found through artistic experience rather than through social integration says a great deal about the place granted to aesthetic values in this universe: they are the only truly motivating values to be found.

Artists

If stigmatized people become artists, similarly, all those who wish to become artists are cursed, excluded, stigmatized: actors who run from audition to audition, writers who run from publisher to publisher, screenwriters who run from producer to producer, musicians who form bands, painters who seek inspiration

and deal with gallery directors. One need not look far to find
an autobiographical thread implicit in these representations.

Le palais des merveilles

Arthur and Annie met at the McDonalds in Créteil. She
was working a cash register. He fell in love. An amateur
writer, he develops a screenplay from their story. Arthur is
kind, but a bit naive. When he learns that his pal Antoine,
a sweet-natured thief, has to go down to the Cannes film
festival to deliver a Jaguar, he is persuaded that this is the
chance he's been waiting for. In Cannes you run into producers on every street corner. And his screenplay is terrific.
Annie told him so.

[Once he's in Cannes, getting into the Palais des Festivals is more difficult than he anticipated. He ends up staying
with many young people in the same situation.] There's a
party going on in the apartment: bottles of booze and cups
lie around everywhere, a sea of tipsy faces. Antoine dances
like a fool. A figure appears wearing an old raincoat, unkempt hair. It's Joseph, a stuttering pickpocket who hangs
around parties announcing to whoever wants to listen that
the end of the world is at hand. In the kitchen filled with
dirty dishes, Arthur talks about his screenplay: "It's the story
of a guy who falls madly in love with a girl." Those listening
are half-interested.

[And in the end, after many misadventures:]

Antoine waves around the attaché case that Arthur has
left behind and throws it out the window. It breaks open
on the sidewalk from the impact and the screenplay scatters
all over. Arthur ponders the pages without the least emotion
and leads Annie away toward the Croisette without saying
a word. Outside, all is calm, one can hear the murmuring
of the surf, there's a full moon. Arthur and Annie head for
the paddle boats on the deserted beach, take one, push it
into the water, and begin peddling into the horizon. Arthur
is full of renewed energy. They make plans for the future:
they'll open a pizzeria, a small clothing boutique—perhaps

a little tearoom? Arthur, finally confident, raises his nose to the stars and exclaims, "Anything is possible."

Arthur's optimism and good humor are not always shared. Things are often taken more seriously. These texts have significant titles: *Au départ, c'est dur; L'important, c'est d'y croire et quand on n'y croit plus, de faire semblant d'y croire; L'espoir qu'un jour!* Artistic careers are surely a means of escaping a lower social class by making precarious, menial jobs a stepping stone to something else, for artistic careers appear as the only possible chance for social climbing, since opportunities for promotion through work seem very limited. But the life of an artist is above all the only desirable means to rise above one's station in life: it is striking that the life of an artist is the only career that is treated as a vocation. Characters do not seek to embrace other causes: the humanitarian is completely absent, as are political involvements, not to mention religion. Art is therefore the only thing that enables one to look beyond the horizon. From the point of view of the characters art is the only quest that justifies a true personal investment, an escape from the general atmosphere of uninvolvement.

La queue

David is an actor, around thirty years old. Out of work. Has odd jobs to get by. Like all his friends. During the day they all zone out in jobs whose only virtue is to keep those who can stand them alive: working at fast-food joints, wearing crepe paper hats and grotesque uniforms; standing at red lights to distribute brochures for car radios, car alarms. All those necessary objects of contemporary life.

Sometimes it's fun, it makes for a second life. Except, in the long term . . .

Every evening it's the same story, the same liberating madness. The apartment has many rooms. And everywhere . . . actors. Some are reciting, others reading, standing up or in an improvised setting, or standing again, motionless, as if for an oratorio. Costumes made out of sheets or curtains from the house. Settings, accessories, suggested: arm-chairs, tables, kitchen utensils, knives, glasses. Above a table a ceiling lamp is throwing a harsh light. (. . .)

Elsewhere, readings and games continue. In every corner of the apartment actors are concentrating on their work. In this labyrinth of light and shadow, they brush against each other, look for each other, forget each other, lose each other. It is an orgy of words, gestures, looks, and movements. A jerry-built and artisanal retreat where heart is everywhere. Fragments of the human experience scattered in the night. After this long voyage everyone goes their own way, ready to endure the day until the next evening when they will be able to exalt once again. They must resist. Hold on. There is the secret hope that one day, luck will come.

For success is completely arbitrary. Fifteen scenarios, all cut almost exactly from the same cloth, tell a certain story: a young man (or young woman), from a very modest background, arrives in Paris. Against the advice of his parents, he seeks a career as an artist (theater, painting, writing, sculpture). All his attempts to break into the artistic milieu fail. He is brutally rejected on several occasions, until the time when, through the greatest of luck, a qualified person discovers his work, understands that he is a genius, and enables him to rise to the greatest heights of his art. But what is striking each time is the completely arbitrary nature of this acknowledgment. We are caught in complete relativism: it is chance that determines success. It comes as it might well not have come, without any external acknowledgment of an intrinsic value. The heart of artistic experience is solitary.

Music

Yet all the arts are not equivalent, and a somewhat unique place is granted to music, music in the pure state, freed of the impurities of the social. For music is everywhere in the universe of the synopses. It concentrates elements within itself that one finds in other art forms—painting, sculpture, literature—but it transcends them by proposing a more accomplished version of them. Obviously, music is the only thing that is truly worthwhile. It is music that establishes communion, relationships, while we are wary of all organized forms of expression. Screenplays devoted to music vibrate with accents that are found nowhere else in the corpus: solemnity, motivation, respect. In fantastic texts, music is associated with the beyond, with death, with eternity. In fact, music takes responsibility for the metaphysical and mystical dimension that is absent from this universe of the screenplays.

But at the same time we find ourselves questioning the significance of that dimension. Music allows characters to short-circuit speech and suggests a disenchantment with words, which is clearly one of the important threads running through the material: a muted disqualification of anything related to a political discourse, distrust of ordinary communication, defiance against amorous discourse. Music proposes a fusional experience for a culture that would finally be rid of the weight of language. But why should we beware of words?

THE MEDIA

There is not just music on the sound track of these thousand screenplays. There is also another noise, that of the media. We are accustomed to hearing that the media are on trial. This is largely transmitted by the press and generally examined by journalists themselves: it always revolves around the issue of their *power*.

Yet in our synopses the debate is not at all set forth around that issue. For the media are not the supports of organized information, the content of which might be challenged: they are dealt with as background noise. The issue that is raised is thus not the greater or lesser importance of the handling of the news; it is how the continual flow of unstructured words and the effect of saturation, of soft indifference, and of demobilization that result from it are managed. We are in fact dealing with how the media are received, and not how they produce. Subsequently, journalists are not in a position of power, in the place where

they happily place themselves (which turns out to be rather fortunate for them when we consider the way in which authors
deal with people in power.) In the world of the synopses, the
media are not manipulators, they are invaders.

The whole issue that develops here is that of the media's
intrusion into the heart of private life. Certain texts take a literal
approach, and show the mountains of newspapers that invade
homes. A rather strange fable tells the story of an incestuous
couple, a brother and sister, who are locked up in a tower with
a collection of newspapers that climbs up to the ceiling.

La manchette

The heirs of Henri Liebmann, newspaper magnate, Margot
and her brother Paul, live as recluses in a huge tower, right
in the center of a large city where for years they have been
piling up the most incredible collection of newspapers from
around the world. They follow the news as closely as possible, joined together by the same passion for news for which
they love each other, hate each other, and tear each other
apart. This exitless scene presents four characters. Margot
and Paul, an incestuous couple obsessed by the search for
truth through their madness as collectors; a refrigerator, the
only connection between the oppression of their interior and
life outside; and the mountain of newspapers, symbol of the
excess information that gradually invades the building, gradually leading this infernal couple to tolerate each other no
longer, and to be separated by the only means possible: death.
      Visual intent of style.
      The inside of the tower must not appear anxiety-pro-
voking, but simply arouse curiosity. The exterior, on the
contrary, must be what it is in reality: noisy, aggressive,
anonymous. Contrary to appearances, hell is not where you
expect to find it.

What is true of the written press is even more so of radio
and television: it is no longer piles of newspapers that climb to

the ceiling, but sound waves that flow in great succession into the intimacy of homes. Many texts use the same rhetorical process to describe this situation: they combine bits of unintelligible sentences from the news with conversations from everyday life. The penetration of the exterior world to the interior of the common language takes into account well the intrusive nature of the media: news terminology is encysted in ordinary communication.

Under the effect of the media the borders between public life and private life are displaced. The two universes penetrate each other. On the one hand the media introduce themselves by breaking into the intimacy of others. On the other hand, the most essential moments of our private lives may become the object of media attention. Any and everybody can therefore at any time find themselves exposing the most crucial moments of their intimacy. Our sorrow, our tears, our anxiety, our death are of the greatest interest to media professionals. For the raw material of news programs is formed from the emotions of others. In the darkest synopses we thus see journalists *thirsting for scoops*, thoughtlessly filming the dying and the dead. In comedies, they intervene in amorous situations: many couples are formed on the air, televised games being the favored scene for this type of arrangement.

We are constantly surprised by the high degree of professional involvement on the part of media professionals. Since we have been used to seeing people unmotivated by their work, the contrast is only that much greater. They are, along with artists, the only ones who demonstrate a true professional consciousness: they are always ready to use their cameras, to jump on their motorcycles, into a moving train to report to the public the news they are missing. They congratulate themselves on the quality of the sound of a convincing sob or of the beautiful image of a well-formed tear. They focus their very sophisticated cameras, their zooms, their wide angles, and are very disappointed when an unanticipated mechanical breakdown causes them to miss the end of a race, or an error in framing, the fall of a jumper. Especially if they can't redo the scene. Such are the risks of live coverage.

According to Erving Goffman,[8] tact consists of sending a person an image that conforms to one that person wishes to emit. At the very least, one could say that the media lack tact: in order to produce an effect they spend their time looking to introduce a maximum distortion between the two images.

The progressive blending of public and private space is conveyed by movements in both directions: on the one hand spectators find themselves exposing the most intimate moments of their private lives, and on the other, media professionals themselves are led to portray publicly the most precious moments of their personal existence.

Norbert, présentateur-télé

Saturday evening, Norbert's show *My Program* resumes. Visibly moved, he has some important news to announce: he has decided to get married on live TV, in front of all the television viewers. The audience holds its breath. The intended is going to come out from behind the curtain. Lydia appears wearing a magnificent dress, in a rain of rose petals. They approach each other, exchange wedding rings in the presence of a priest in full ceremonial dress, who blesses them. A choir of young singers accompanies them, singing religious songs. Then the apotheosis: a cake in their image is brought out onto the stage. They are cheered. All of this bodes well for the future of the station and gives more ideas to the boss and to his faithful collaborator, who is for once smiling. Mr. Maurice, who has just returned, is appreciative: "Now that's television!"

Norbert whispers to his wife: "What are we going to do next week?"

The media are intrusive. But it has become very difficult to do without them. Some characters are innovative and find original solutions to protect themselves, like Protz and Schmutz

---

8. Erving Goffman, *The Presentation of Self in Everyday Life* (Garden City, N.Y., 1959).

who, tired of contemplating the misfortunes of others, have developed their own TV show.

Protz et Schmutz tv

Emil Protz and Bob Schmutz were Boy Scouts together. They have been living together for . . . let's say a long time. When they aren't trying to have fun at each other's expense, they do so at others people's expense. They love TV, but they prefer TV that resembles them. They therefore buy a video camera and plan to produce the first home TV. They name it "Protz and Schmutz TV." They will be the producers and the only viewers.

Then there are Jean and Lisa, who go into the TV set, as punishment (*Les déchaînés*), and Jean-Jacques, who has abandoned writing his novel to sell television sets and falls into a deep sleep as soon as a television is turned on: a good way to protect oneself from troublesome images. It's just a bit of a pity that it happens at the precise moment when he manages to get the most ravishing of baby-sitters into his bed (*L'histoire ordinaire*).

The Rules of the Social Game

We can now enlarge the framework of our reflections, for we know enough to understand how this imagined world is organized and what traits cause a character to be truly harmful.

Obviously, those who are at the top of the social hierarchy are viewed the worst. But this is because they have everything at once: it is they who have the most money, the most knowledge, the most power, the largest number of relationships. They accumulate all resources, but at the same time all the elements are confused in their hands. To view things more clearly and to know what the truly determining criteria in the hierarchy of values really are, we must therefore descend all the steps of the pyramid one by one: gradually we see the issues are differentiated. There in fact remain disagreeable characters in clearly less enviable social positions.

If you win the lottery, if you discover a treasure, if you win on a TV game show, if the ATM in which you have slipped your card goes crazy, or if you are immensely successful at a well-prepared burglary, you can become rich without automatically shifting to the side of the bad guys. That might signify a sort of state of grace, one that enables those who have had good luck to have the opportunity to enjoy freely the fruits of their good fortune. Those lucky ones are thus miraculously spared the disapproval that usually accompanies the rich. An exceptional fate for an exceptional situation. But money that falls from the sky by chance is not the only windfall to be accepted: there is also that which comes from an inheritance. There are many heroes who in the course of a story benefit from an expected or unexpected inheritance that greatly improves their financial situation. Here, too, our authors allow them to profit serenely from that gift.

These exceptions are important: they show that money is not always stigmatizing. Characters can be both rich and good. But on one condition: that they did not acquire their riches from work. This might signify that what differentiates protagonists is not wealth, but rather their relationship to work. Indeed, when we look again at the list of positive and negative characters, we notice that quite often what distinguishes them is their having a job: the homeless, the ill, the down-and-out, retirees, children on the one hand; developers, managers of supermarkets, executives in advertising agencies, lawyers, judges, doctors on the other. This might explain the particular animosity shown toward bureaucrats: if they are ignorant to such a degree, it is essentially because they benefit from the security of a job. Conversely, a dynamic and arrogant young executive abruptly becomes good when, overnight, he finds himself out of work. Many texts begin with the day when the hero, having become aware of the absurdity of his existence, suddenly leaves a job that earned him a decent living, in which he often invested a lot of energy, to go in search of himself: to abandon one's work willingly is a way to become worthy of sympathy. Here, too, however, there are certain exceptions: first-generation immigrants are defined by their position in the workforce, yet they remain positive figures. But there is another category that can work as much as they like without being discredited for it: artists. Painters, sculptors, musicians, writers, and poets appear quite often in the synopses. Now, if they are of course presented as inspired creators, they are also diligent workers who devote themselves entirely to their profession, night and day, without interruption, in a time frame that is not marked by the social rhythms of alternating work and rest. Ascetics, they sacrifice all other pleasures in life to their profession. Perfectionists, they untiringly put their works back on the drawing board. The motivation is as strong in amateurs as in professionals. All of them can spend their days in their workshops or seated at their pianos, go through galleries and cocktail parties, experience the pain of creation or the giddiness of success, they are always characters endowed with immense prestige. But isn't this because they escape a hierarchical position: they have neither superiors nor subordinates, and their work, like their success, is carried out in zones protected from the ordinary exercise of power.

This is why it seems that the true dividing line that separates positive characters from negative ones is rather the axis of power. Indeed, this line of demarcation does not appear to be contradicted, and it deals perfectly with all the conflicting interpretations that have been encountered up to now. This is why drug addicts are sympathetic, but dealers odious, prostitutes alluring, but pimps atrocious, young Arabs are positive except when they are the (tyrannical) brothers of their sisters, etc. The axis goes inside the margins to divide up the characters within. Thus, if we listen carefully to the ultimate message conveyed by all the synopses put together, we would hear that unanimous call to defiance against the power exercised by others.

But we would have to look closer at exactly what type of power is in question. It is not power linked to birth: there are indeed a few very decadent aristocrats here and there, but the fact that they are relegated along with their trained domestics to the strange chateaux of fantastic texts indicates their unrealistic status. And above all, their numbers are not large enough for them to be granted much importance. It is not really hierarchical power that is exercised in the spheres of professional life, since there is scarcely any professional life anymore, and consequently, not much hierarchical power anymore. (That said, the power that does endure is obviously ill viewed.) Nor is it technological power: technical objects obtained their autonomy a long time ago, and we saw earlier that they got along very well all alone in a world without humans. In any event, we are in a universe where the characters are little concerned with the accomplishment of great edifying technological works. Neither bridges nor highways nor locomotives are built. There are scarcely any engineers, entrepreneurs, workers, or technicians. Finally, it is not the technocratic power of institutions, since they, as we have seen, are completely overwhelmed: they are still able to impose small annoyances, but scarcely anything else. Institutions no longer attempt to constrain personalities within the framework of large totalitarian companies. They would indeed be incapable of doing so. *In fact, the power at issue is one that manifests a direct hold over the body or mind of the other.* This is why it can come from very diverse sources, be exercised from the top to the bottom of the social hierarchy, create a divide in the very heart of the margins. A garage mechanic destroys your car, a hairdresser ruins your hair. The repairman comes to your home and ruins all of your household appliances. The most archaic forms are not the least frightening (one must especially beware of witches). But each time it is a strictly *individual* power, a power of each person over another person, a power that is no longer connected to any great machine. A direct, stripped-down power, since all the intermediary bodies, all the counterpowers, all the instances that might constitute relays or places of arbitration, have been liquidated: there are no associations, no political parties, no unions. All of the connective tissue has been destroyed. If there are no mediations, nor are there any recognized regulations. We are in a world where the law is completely distorted: the laws serve the powerful, and the lawyers serve to thwart the laws. The judicial framework itself no longer offers any protection. Society has come undone. It can no longer be held together. The crisis of institutions has engendered a crisis of the bonds that connect us.

＼Three

Intimacies

W e will now leave the realm of the social and enter into that of the psychological. However, we will not witness a significant difference: the same tendency toward *deinstitutionalization* is at work with regard to personal relationships—with the same consequences. Here, too, we note a lack of any admitted rules or instances of regulation. Anything can happen. Nothing is certain. No relationship is stable. Because of this, the home does not provide a refuge against the difficulties of existence, a space where one can retreat to regain strength and to confront the complications of life in a more serene setting. It is not a place that provides confidence and reparation because it is traversed by the same issues and undermined by the same contradictions as the social space. Thus, instead of serving as contrasts, these two universes echo each other. This is why life is so hard in the world of the synopses.

Now, what interests the authors is no longer describing strongly stereotypical characters, rather it is analyzing models of the relationships that connect them (parents/children, men/women, grandparents/grandchildren). Individuals have the same type of social characteristics, and their sociological environment is not very different. But these givens then become secondary, for the plot is focused on the interpersonal dimension of the action and not on its social dimension. What was in the forefront on the public stage is moved to the background on the private stage.

In the past twenty years familial structures have been deeply transformed: the drop in the birthrate, the drop in the number of marriages, the rise in the number of divorces, the increased number of unmarried couples, the explosion of births out of wedlock, the push toward celibacy, the rise of solitude—these are the many phenomena that have radically changed the general context of family life. With some distance behind us, we now know that the typical family of the 1960s, comprised of two married parents and their children, which formed the usual reference to the ideal family, was in fact but a short moment in our history.

As Louis Roussel reminds us in *La famille incertaine*,[1] the family is less and less of an institution: it has rid itself of the social constraints that weighed upon it and now rests completely on the affective dimension, on feeling. Every institution separates and organizes, creating order through the game of classifications that it creates. The traditional familial institution guaranteed

The separation of generations by assigning specific functions to each age;

The differentiation between the sexes by giving men and women different roles;

The organization of the social exercise of paternity.

Whether the order that resulted from this was just or unjust, whether it came from nature or from the culture—or from both at the same time—does not concern us here. What we wish to know is how the characters in the synopses react to this vast movement of *deinstitutionalization* occurring within the family, what consequences are derived from that movement as the characters function in their private lives, and how the characters manage these new uncertainties.

In truth, they don't manage very well. We must immediately point out that it is the authors themselves who cast a disillusioned look on the situations they describe. They emphasize their value judgments with depreciating adjectives. What distin-

---

1. Louis Roussel, *La famille incertaine* (Paris, 1989).

guishes their words from those of a reactionary position, however (the family has always been at the center of polemics, and
the notion of the crisis of the family is a very ideologically loaded
one), is that their gloomy statements regarding an interpersonal
disintegration are never accompanied by a will to restore an old
order, nor by utopian perspectives for radical transformations:
the family is no longer to be overthrown. It is already very
beaten down.

THE DECOMPOSED FAMILY

Although many stories focus on the problems of private life, the
family is rarely central to a plot. It is rarely present as a structured, hierarchized entity with a clear identity and familiar rituals, meals, family holidays, marriages, anniversaries. (Generally,
moreover, the theme of food is notably absent from the synopses.) Nor are there activities shared in common: sports, leisure
activities, vacations.

The traditional theme of the threat posed by someone who
through his escapades or his passions might threaten the internal cohesion of the group is missing. For the group no longer
has any true cohesion. Its members are not connected by a bond
of visceral solidarity that goes beyond individual antagonisms.
The very term *member* appears devoid of meaning. The family
as social cell is dead.

Nothing else remains but interindividual problematic relationships. In fact, like a beam from a projector, the synopses
highlight one aspect or another of familial relationships: some
are centered on the problems of the couple, fatherhood, the
mother-child relationship, sibling bonds. But each segment is
dealt with in isolation, and there is no central place or a privileged moment when these diverse elements are combined or
confronted. In any event, in general the heroes of these texts
spend more time outside their homes than with members of
their own families. Nor is there any reference to any sort
of family values. Family relationships are a simple variation of
other forms of relationships. Gradually, the psychologizing of

relationships has won out over an affirmation of the specificity of interpersonal bonds.

The family dynamics represented in the screenplays are therefore the exact opposite of those portrayed on television through television hosts, one that they reaffirm in variety programs: the host is always presented in the midst of a unified, solid, and solidary family, a secure refuge against the difficulties of life. No amount of rhetoric is spared to glorify the warmth of the home, the pleasures of the table, and the joys of intimacy, as they constantly reaffirm the primacy of the family values whose true function is to reassure its members.[2]

But we are also poles apart from the imaginary world of *Dallas*. For under the fiery Texan sun *Dallas* presents the sibling rivalries and conjugal dramas that unfold on the backdrop of a powerful and unshakable familial structure. The clan rivalries of intertwined kinship weave an impregnable network. JR's infamies never go beyond the rules of biological solidarity involving heirs or descendants. In fact, the vicissitudes of the Ewing family constantly show that individual affective issues and issues of family loyalties are played out on different levels.[3]

THE BLENDING OF GENERATIONS

The way the succession of generations is portrayed in the synopses evokes a club sandwich: different generations are all piled up; each one is assigned a negative or positive value; the good alternate with the bad—one fresh, one rotten—harmonious relationships are woven between alternate generations. In this layout the intermediary generation, that of the parents of young adults, forms a generation that is quite ill viewed. And we have seen in the tables at the beginning of this work, moreover, that that generation is underrepresented.

But a point must be stressed from the outset. Whereas in the section dealing with social representations, differences in

2. Sabine Chalvon-Demersay and Dominique Pasquier, *Drôles de stars: La télévision des animateurs* (Paris, 1990), and "Le langage des variétés" *Terrain* 15 (1990).

3. Elihu Katz and Tamar Liebes, "Six interprétations de la série *Dallas*," *Hermès*, 11–12 April 1993; Florence Dupont, *Homère et Dallas* (Paris, 1990).

the authors' own sociological characteristics did not have any noticeable bearing on the thematics developed in their works, the same is not true here. There is a determining variable— the age of the authors—that intervenes in their choice of subjects and in the way those subjects are treated. Authors who are under thirty-five more readily develop stories that portray their parents' generation. Authors over thirty-five are more interested in young children. And we will see a bit later what is at issue with regard to love stories. In other words, the authors' preoccupations reflect their placement in the cycle of life. They also coincide with a break in the generations. In fact, the authors over thirty-five are in the flow of the large postwar generation, that of the baby boomers and of May '68. They participate in a culture that is spread widely over the public stage, a culture that has difficulty representing to itself the characteristics of its successors in terms that do not denote a deficit or a return to tradition. Those under thirty-five, the majority here (let us recall that six out of ten authors are under thirty-five) belong to a generational culture that is more discreet and less enamored with ready-made formulations.

The parents of young adults do not form a barrier against the difficulties of life: swept along by the trends of modernity and the complications of contemporary life, they are carried along like straws in the wind. They are therefore incapable of serving as anchors or as models of stability.

The relationships they establish with their children are not satisfying, but they are rarely conflictual: children do not leave slamming the door behind them; the conflict between the generations is not expressed through violent explosions (it is couples who monopolize violent quarrels). Obviously, for a conflict to exist parents would have to be seen as representing an established moral and social order: but this is not the case, since parents are completely out of touch. Moreover, they are confronted with the same problems as their children: unemployment, solitude, disappointments in love. But the similarity in the crises endured only manages to separate the two generations, as if children were tacitly reproaching those who preceded them for not having known or found the solutions to their difficulties, nor altered their difficulties by accepting growing old. This leads us into the stark tableau of a generation of parents who are either even more lost than their own children, or completely indifferent, or finally, who live obscure rivalries with them. These three problematic situations serve to express the very strong antagonism that opposes two overly similar generations.

When characters escape that antagonism, the alternative situation is scarcely more attractive: we are then shown the tableau of the extreme egotism of a generation that has rid itself of its predecessors (by putting them in the retirement homes, asylums, or death houses that we have already seen above) and has refused to provide its descendants with any form of affective support. At most, it provides material support in morose silence.

In a single realm, however, parents do abandon their reserve. This is in fact the realm in which they might reasonably abstain: they increasingly intervene in matters concerning the sexuality of their children. They select their children's partners, congratulate themselves on their multiple successes, but are upset with certain choices ("What a fool, what an idiot, poor Laurent!"). They increase their uncalled-for interference and disagreeable meddling. Arnaud has a date with his girlfriend: his mother tearfully calls him and begs him to come see her. She has just broken up with her latest lover and expects him to console her (*Clair obscur*). Or a young girl goes out with some bohemian boys; her father undertakes to hire a gigolo with good manners so he will become her lover (*Entremise*); in *Martin a du style,* a bedridden and tyrannical mother calls the woman her son is interested in all sorts of names, whereas another mother, on the contrary, rejoices in her son's conquests with an incongruous complacency. ("She brings breakfast to the sleeping couple. She is delighted with her son's latest conquest.")

The invasive mother-in-law is an element in the traditional folklore of French vaudeville. But here is an example of one who undoubtedly goes beyond all imaginable limits. "Mysterious bonds seem to join the mother and son, like those of an eternal couple: Iris is too devoted to the young couple to be sincere, she never stops meddling in their lives, in their apartment, and Pascale discovers that she lives right across the hall. (. . .) She has the feeling that Iris wants to take her place, penetrate her corporal envelope, become young again and live with Laurent" (*Double exposition*).

Many texts even suggest an incestuous deviation. They can be interpreted from an anthropological perspective, as a supplementary element in the development of the theme of crises of interpersonal bonds.

The theme of the erasing of generational boundaries, which is aided by increased longevity and a new elasticity in the roles assigned to different stages in life, leads to the emergence of new forms of rivalries.

Indeed, a certain number of texts portray a competition between the generations in the sexual or matrimonial marketplace. We are shown either an indirect rivalry—couples are formed with partners of widely varying ages: a mature woman goes out with a young boy; a middle-aged man with a young girl—which in a traditional society would have inspired a wonderful charivari. But in the society of the synopses, this is the only solution that somewhat neutralizes the unbearable rivalries between men and women. The situation becomes even more troubling when parents and children begin to fish from the same waters: parents choose their own partners from their children's group of friends. Sometimes the competition occurs right in the midst of the family: the mother flirts outrageously with her daughter's young lover. The father loves his son's wife. Some adventures go rather far: a young woman, a photographer in Barcelona, falls in love with a man, then with the father of that man, with whom she will have a baby, who will in fact be the half brother of her husband, who will know nothing: his "son" looks like him (*La preuve par sang*).

Problematic Fatherhood

Whereas the mass media, with their great supply of resounding reports and thundering articles, have informed us about the emergence of a category of men unknown up to now—the new fathers—a very different situation was developing silently in the background. The synopses have indeed picked up on this. We do see a few fathers, here and there, raising their child alone, like Marc in *Le rouge et le vert:* "Marc is the handsome guy in the workplace, always comfortable and so rushed that his colleagues suspect a life filled with female conquests. Marc lets this legend develop, while in reality he's hiding a secret: he's raising his son Valentin."

But more often texts tell the story of a confiscated fatherhood. First, men have a lot of difficulty convincing their wives to have a child, mainly because the wives have other priorities.

Clair obscur

> PAUL: I want to have a child with you! Yes, a child. A boy or a girl, whatever you'd like. Don't be so against a new life!
> FRANCINE: Paul, I want you to understand, to know.
> PAUL: There's only one thing I want—give me a child, I'm begging you, right away!
> FRANCINE: My career, Paul, think of my career. You're not thinking.

The couple would also have to remain committed to their plan for a long time, which does not always appear to be the case.

La brèche

> PIERRE: We spend wonderful evenings together, it's uncomplicated, it's great, it's complete, now you tell me that makes you want to have a baby with me.
> MURIEL: What's wrong with that?
> PIERRE: It's really touching.
> MURIEL: I don't see what you don't understand.
> PIERRE: I don't know, when I come over to see you, your life seems to be so full. You seem to be doing so well. I thought you wanted to have a baby all alone.

Then there's the man who must live through the pregnancy of his partner. He becomes transformed into a "father-to-be filled with fears and doubts," confronted with a "woman whose pregnancy and belly, which looks like a hot-air balloon, occupy her full-time." This is also recounted in the form of a comedy in *Grossesse nerveuse*.

Then the baby arrives. Very often the couple has already drifted apart. In many texts the women have their babies alone, in unlikely places, dark, comical, or dramatic: "In a little chapel, without a clinic or epidural, in the midst of thunder and lightening. And this to the great joy of the young mother who would never have dreamed of such a grandiose culmination to her personal adventure. Eric is very far away, distanced. He arrives after the battle. He isn't sure he'll ever be able to make up the delay" (*Cado*).

A true uncertainty might weigh on the origins of the child.

Si c'était lui, ce ne sera pas moi

ANDRÉ: Who was Marie's father?

VÉRONIQUE: Someone I met on a trip. It's no one's business.

ANDRÉ: Not even Marie's?

VÉRONIQUE: I would have given anything not to have known my father!

ANDRÉ: Excuse me, but how about him, Marie's father?

VÉRONIQUE: He took advantage of the situation, like I did. He didn't ask for anything else, like me. Anyway, we're not in the nineteenth century anymore!

ANDRÉ: It's weird. So you can have children without knowing it.

This uncertainty itself can become a formidable dramatic springboard:

Doutes d'hiver

A couple without a history; the wife, Pia, around thirty years old, pregnant, leaves for a few days on business. The man, Pacôme, goes back to bed. A doorbell rings. A woman, Gisèle, a former girlfriend, with topaz blue eyes, is standing at the door. Surprise. He invites her in. She sits down, and he finds himself in a delicate, equivocal situation. The neighbor comes to borrow a drill, the door is left open; a telephone call from his in-laws . . . She shares his breakfast. That evening they go to the movies together, then begin the confidences: she tells him that after they broke up she had a child to whom she gave his name, Pacôme. "Panicked, and believing he is being trapped, Pacôme pretends to be indifferent, avoiding every indiscreet question that might indicate he is the father, while Gisèle maliciously allows doubt to hang over him. While considering his chances of being beyond suspicion, he considers the damage this huge delayed bomb will undoubtedly create in his life."

With fathers being thus excluded, or excluding themselves, many children go looking for them. While they are little, children are content to question those around them: Sarah is making sand castles on a beach in Brittany. She asks questions of her aunt, who remains evasive: "So wasn't my daddy even a Martian? You must have talked to him a few times, didn't you?" (*Caravane*).

A bit later they want to know more:

La fugue

Edouardo, a fourteen-year-old boy, leaves home. He leaves his mother, but especially Christian, the man she's living with. He goes looking for his father. "For the one who caused his conception. His mother met him in Switzerland, at a ski resort, before he was born, when she was a waitress in Switzerland. He knows his name is Edouardo, too. He uncovered the pay stubs from the restaurant where his mother used to work, more than fourteen years ago. He wants to find him." Christian will follow him discreetly, quietly, picking up his trail with the help of information provided by the ATMs where the boy takes out money.

We are far from the popular novel of the nineteenth century where the voice of blood immediately makes itself heard and where the culmination of the search enables the lost or abandoned child to regain his place in the bosom of a wealthy family. The family novel continues, but the epilogue has been changed: reunions are devastating. At best the child spends a day with an incredulous father who, when the evening comes, explains that the child must return home, for he doesn't belong there. At worst he discovers that his father is a weapons dealer, that he manages a prostitution ring, "that he is a man apparently above all suspicion, who has officially made his fortune in scrap iron, but has been a drug trafficker for more than twenty-five years." Or, elsewhere: "a trafficker of children under the guise of humanitarian work." The search for a father almost always ends up in disillusion.[4]

MEN AND WOMEN

Nothing works anymore between men and women. Quite often a synopsis begins with a breakup:

4. There is an awareness here of the paternity crisis in contemporary society that rests both on a situation of fact and on a situation of law. In 1991, one child out of three was born out of wedlock, and in such cases the mother alone had parental authority, even if the father recognized the child as his and the baby had his name; a judicial situation of which fathers only became aware at the time of a possible breakup. In fact, these measures were established within a very different context: the year was 1972, within a very stable familial model, with 6 percent of all births out of wedlock; legislators were concerned with ensuring a certain continuity for the child. In their opinion, if the father wanted to obtain part of his parental authority, he had only to marry the mother. It was at that time unimaginable that there could be mothers who did not want to be married.

Moreover, the number of divorces in France has stabilized to around one hundred thousand per year. In 85 percent of the cases the mother is awarded custody of the children, in 9 percent the father gains custody, with joint or alternate custody representing around 6 percent of all cases. Henri Léridon and Catherine Villeneuve Gokalp, with Laurent Toulmon, in *Constance et inconstances de la famille: Biographies familiales des couples et des enfants,* Travaux et documents, no. 134, PUF-INED,1994, have revealed that in practice divorce has often been accompanied by a break in the relationship of the child with the noncustodial parent. Child support is paid irregularly and relationships become more distant. In 1985, at the time of the survey, 13 percent of the children of divorced parents lived with their fathers, 18 percent saw them frequently, 27 percent once or twice a month, 23 percent less than once a month, and 20 percent no longer at all ("Entre père et mère," *Population et sociétés,* INED, 220, June 1988).

L'entracte

> *The screen is black. A door opens onto a Paris street.*

> VOICE OFF: This is me. I'm leaving my wife.

The separation is depicted at the start. It is not the culmination of a long process of decline that is described in minute detail throughout the text; on the contrary, it constitutes the preamble to it:

> 11:30 A.M. Jean-Jacques, a man of twenty-five or twenty-six, a failed writer, wakes up with a hangover. His girlfriend dumped him during the night, leaving a message on his typewriter. (*Secteur d'enfer*).

The reader is not the only one to be surprised by the abruptness of the separation; the partner in the separated couple also seems caught off guard: he wakes up alone in the morning and finds his bed empty, his apartment deserted, the keys in his mailbox.

A woman comes home and sees a moving van:

Une petite ville bien tranquille

> LESLIE: Fred . . . Fred, are you here?

> *Leslie quickly takes out her glasses and puts them on. The TV is gone from the TV table. There are marks on the walls left from pictures that have been removed. The sofa has disappeared, but the two little tables that were around it lie upended on the ground; some records, but no stereo. Leslie walks on something, bends down and picks up some keys. She compares them with hers: they are identical. (. . .)*

> LESLIE: And not a note! He didn't even leave a note. Gone like a thief in the night!

When the synopses allow us a slightly longer look at the difficulties encountered in the course of a shared life, the problems presented are more about the distribution of tasks in everyday life than about stories of jealousy ("At home, everyone does their own dishes, refuses to wash the other person's laundry, etc."). It is as if certain conflicts were more legitimate than others and could therefore be more easily portrayed. The life of a traditional couple does not appear uplifting, punctuated as it is by boredom, moroseness, and lassitude, "the stereotypical life of a couple, a life worn down by conjugal habits and duties." And the life of a more modern couple is shown dotted with quarrels: "One autumn evening, around 9:00 P.M., Victor is fighting with his girlfriend, Alice, about the shopping that wasn't done and a dinner that wasn't prepared. He goes out into a pouring rain; the scene is viewed from outside the building through venetian blinds whose slats are slightly opened." Crisis situations are evoked briefly or, on the contrary, detailed with great delight: an entire synopsis is devoted to listing the endless insults that a man and a woman inflict upon each other. "The days go by and the dirty tricks continue." But often, in a more radical way, it is the difficulties of communication within the couple that are brought to the fore. They are particularly well illustrated in the form the separation assumes: a breakup without warning and without appeal.

Et pourtant la Seine coule

Olivier believes in his life, which is dominated by success, including his love for Cécile. She informs him of her departure overseas, an extraordinary promotion, which cannot be turned down. She wants to go alone, to succeed, and anyway, "they weren't doing so well as a couple," she says. He doesn't understand, he wants to know, there must be something else, because he wasn't aware of any problem. Cécile: "Yes, that's just it. We never talked to each other." She leaves.

These early separations enable the hero to regain his original availability, so he will be ready for new adventures: it is only once the breakup is complete that the story can truly begin. But these separations also have another meaning. In fact, the crisis described is not merely one that the hero endures; it also represents a sort of symbolic putting to death of the very notion of "couple." The hero leaves his former relationship the way one gets rid of an uncomfortable and outmoded outfit.

If the couple is doing so badly, it is because the relationship between men and women has changed: men are weak, and women are domineering. For the authors of the screenplays, the relationship between the sexes has not been marked by a general movement toward an equalizing of positions: the situation has in fact shifted completely round. We have gone directly, without any transition, from male oppression to female domination. And this is seen in manuscripts written by women as well as in those written by men.

Men are weak and timid ("Philippe's eyes, one blue, the other brown, are like the sky on the verge of tears"). Women are beautiful (not pretty, but beautiful), sensual, but venal and domineering. They make the decisions, work too much ("yuppies and carnivores"), take charge of the amorous relationship ("religious lover"), maintain social relationships. One could make a list of all the forms of domination they exercise over their helpless partners. There is psychological domination: they are stronger and better able to cope with difficult circumstances ("She calms the panicked voice of her man on the other end of the line, she implores him to buck up"); intellectual domination: they are more successful in their studies, therefore have more degrees, are more cultivated; professional domination: they invest more in their job and have little difficulty triumphing over their demobilized partners; and family domination: they have always had it, and it's unthinkable that they would give it up. If this tableau were limited to the new middle layers of society, to the intersection of a social class and a generation, we would not be surprised to see the profound consequences of the feminist movements depicted thus. But feminine power spills beyond these bounds: it also involves previous generations (mothers are abusive and tyrannical, and grandmothers are strong) and extends to various social milieus. In fact, one has the feeling that the women in the synopses draw on all resources simultaneously, in that they continue to hold onto the usual means of conjugal manipulation used by women in traditional couples, and to these have added new methods of control born out of the women's lib movement. All of this occurs in a climate of age-old revenge: billions of women oppressed since the beginning of humanity have not yet been avenged.

There are, of course, differences depending on the social groups that are represented, but the power relationship is in fact never very different; it is the way in which that relationship unfolds and the foundations upon which it rests that vary. In more modest social environments women often display an ardent desire for social promotion that is not often shared by a partner who seems satisfied with the mediocrity of his situation. "She chides her husband for keeping company with disreputable types and for not having any social ambition. She would like to move to a more fashionable neighborhood, but her husband refuses" (*Le Canari bleu*). They try to push their husbands toward other goals: "Vincent works as a mechanic in a garage in town and has no desire for anything else. It quickly becomes apparent that Claire reproaches him for this lack of ambition, as well as for the fact that he is exploited by his employer" (*Onc' Damien*).

Another theme of discord is the importance women place on their work. ("Early on, he will try to get closer to his wife, who, too busy with her work, will abandon him without even realizing it.") The investment women have in their work is all the more noteworthy in that the notion of work itself is, in general, rather devalued in the synopses. The distance between the sexes is only the greater because of it. "Hélène, graduate of a Grande Ecole, has entered the high-level sector of a ministry where she is carving out a successful career that gives her an opening into the corridors of power. As for Olivier, he finds himself out of the game."

Women have not just seized power in the professional realm, they are also empowered in the most intimate spheres of private life: they often take the initiative in amorous relationships. ("Martin, awkward, resists the advances of the young woman.") They pick men up: "Muriel is in a nightclub. She unwinds by dancing. She looks at the men, chooses one of them, and dances with him in a provocative way. She brings him home with her and sleeps with him. When they are done, she asks him to leave." One might believe that it is experience acquired in these realms that gives them such assurance. But not at all—beginners demonstrate an equal determination:

Le choix d'aimer

Sonia has just turned twenty-three and has decided to "skip a step" and finally make up for a delay that was somewhat weighing on her. She envisions the situation as a formality, and any young and healthy man will do, since she has no intention of falling in love. She has therefore set aside eight days to become a woman and to finish up with that "concern." [She meets Patrick, tall, well built, nice in spite of appearing somewhat common, which suggests to her that he is from a modest background. The affair is concluded, she thought she was going to get rid of him, but he becomes attached to her. After making him more presentable,] Sonia, satisfied with "her work," nevertheless wonders what she will do with him. For at that moment Patrick is of no more interest to her. She has finished playing, and he no longer amuses her.

Women use a traditionally masculine vocabulary ("I think you're really cute"), make declarations and marriage proposals, and possess a certain number of virile attributes. And they should be seen behind the wheel: they drive their cars the way they conduct their lives—without restraint.

Papillons en folie

Sophie behind the wheel of her red coupe. Claude guides her, frightened by her driving.
She leans too far over toward him.

SOPHIE: Oh, Claude, you smell so good!
CLAUDE (straightening the steering wheel): Hey, watch out, please, look at the road!

SOPHIE: You're afraid, my pet? Say, does it bother you that
    I call you "pet"?
CLAUDE: Look out for the baby carriage!
SOPHIE: It's OK. I saw it. You don't need to yell at me, my
    pet. Do we have far to go?

There is a type of relationship that ends up with a certain
definition of the ideal man: "Richard is exactly the type of man
who makes his woman happy. He is always ready to prepare a
feast for his beloved when she comes home exhausted from her
job."

This can reach extreme situations: in one text we see a
woman reduce her lover to nothing more than a capricious and
irresponsible child. In another, he actually turns into a woman:

Pygmalionnes

In a chic old-time pub Marianne, Carmen, and Sophie are drinking
beer and talking about men. "Cynical, they can't help voicing a few
virulent judgments against guys: always macho, egotistical, infantile,
cumbersome. And such bad lovers, most of the time." They will pick
up a hitchhiker, a "nice and naive angelic blond young man," who
is heading to Paris to look for work. They put him up and then decide
to educate him in order to turn him into an ideal lover and companion, "shaped according to their demands." That is, "nice, available,
tender when necessary, a psychologist, attentive, a music lover,
too." The women dress him, fix his hair, teach him to prepare easy
dishes and healthy cocktail parties.

They are delighted with the exemplary performances of their pupil-
lover. Until the day when the young man, caught up in the logic of
his new role, begins to dress like a woman and declares to them
that "thanks to them and to their instruction he has understood that
he is happier and truly himself in adopting a feminine life and appearance." Carmen is flabbergasted. Marianne breaks down,
bursts into tears, and finds solace in a bottle of whisky: "They want
a man, not a woman!"

The beautiful Marianne's cry of despair is undoubtedly
representative of her ambivalence. These women pay the

price of their contradictory demands: they have trouble being satisfied with the loss of virility that they have nevertheless imposed. The new male weakness in ultimately quite intolerable. The new interchangeability of roles and functions creates a period of flux and of uncomfortable indetermination. To get out of it one resorts to known models: the partner becomes either feminized, or infantilized. As if there were no other means to escape the confusion than resorting to clearly identified, already existing roles, those of a child, or of a woman.

The Ideal Woman

It is therefore not very surprising that in this difficult context a certain number of main characters go in search of the ideal woman. The most intriguing quest is certainly this one:

Syn pour la vie

A young student, extremely talented in computer science, decides to construct the robot-portrait of the ideal woman on his computer by giving her the intelligence of Marie Curie and the beauty of Ava Gardner—and other things, as well: "Serge, alone, shut up in the computer room. In front of him, a photo of the Venus of Milo, arms cut out of *Playboy*, a profile of a black woman, a mouth, magnificent eyes . . . a girl wearing white anklets, the knees, the ankles of a Eurasian, etc. But thinking also of the "intellect" side, he introduces the complete works of Marguerite Duras, the essays of Françoise Giroud, the biography of Eleanor of Aquitaine, and the works of Benoîte Groult."

Being overly successful in his scientific undertaking, he loses his fiancée and finds himself pulled by his superb and perfect creation into the bowels of the computer. Fortunately, all ends well. His best friend saves him from the clutches of the synthetic woman, and he is put into the arms of his friend's sister, "with whom he will be able to create small creatures of his dreams, but this time using purely human means."

Sexuality

Sex is very prevalent, infinitely more so than one is allowed to depict on television in a TV movie shown during prime time. It is unbridled, even though there is no synopsis that is truly pornographic. What we see instead are furtive relationships, lived in an atmosphere of extreme urgency. An indication of this urgency is found in the great variety of the locales chosen by lovers to carry out their amorous adventures.

In general, we witness a spectacular shortening of the preliminaries: "Binette, a young student finishing up her studies, meets Ben, also a student, at the university cafeteria. Struck by an abrupt desire for each other, they run to make love in Binette's room. A very simple, very beautiful love story begins, with the employment crisis in the background" (*Ben et Binette*).

Granted, this urgency can be explained in part by the writing constraints placed on the synopses, since the authors have only a few pages to develop their stories—except in general their characters simply will not wait very long. In fact, the sexual relationship is not the culmination of a loving relationship. It can, on the contrary, form the prelude to it, but this is not always the case. Sexual encounters are often one-night stands: the sexual act is often completely detached from feelings or the expression of them.

> He says to her: I don't want you to get attached.
> She bursts out laughing: "If we became attached every time we had a fling!" and reassures him: he believes her (what a generation!) and goes along when she embraces him. (*L'ange-gardien*)

The disassociation of sex from love and marriage is a classic theme of the amorous ideology of our time. More unusual is the fact that sex is disassociated from love to such a degree. It has become so unsentimental and so often venal.

Venality

Recourse to prostitution is extremely common in the synopses. It is a theme that recurs over and over in the texts: for men it is a way to have a woman. For women it is a way to get money. It is as common among girls as delinquency is among boys, and it has become completely commonplace. This frequency and neutrality might appear surprising: how is it that the liberation of mores in this imaginary universe has turned sex into a trade, instead of freeing it from monetary constraints? Is there not some incompatibility between the triumph of loving feelings that has marked our age and explained the entire disintegration of the traditional family system, and the omnipresence of this particular mode of trade between men and women? Finally, how is it that the women who, as we have seen, are so domineering so easily give up their bodies to masculine desire? All of these representations appear completely contradictory. In fact, it must first be stressed that the girls who become prostitutes are not victims (with the exception of a few professionals who would like to leave the sidewalks but who cannot escape their pimps). We have broken with the entire imagery of prostitution that dated from before the sexual revolution: the girls who are prostitutes are not degraded or dishonored (there is only one text in this vein; it is written by a native of North Africa, that is, set within a specific cultural context). Nor are they "the ones whom the goddess Famine one cold winter evening forced to raise their skirts in the streets," ready to sacrifice their honor to save their family and feed their children, etc. In other words, they inspire neither scorn nor pity, two sentiments traditionally found together in the same arena, that of sexual repression and female subordination. Sexuality is no longer inscribed within an economy of honor, but neither is it situated in an economy of eroticism.

In fact, we have the feeling that the venality of sex is a way of leaving behind the contradictions of the current social and ideological system that, on the one hand, imposes the necessity of sexual accomplishment and, on the other, is inscribed in interpersonal difficulties that poison the relationship between men and women. Reduced to a minimal exchange, this form of sexuality respects the feeling of urgency (the sexual act is an abrupt impulse, the fulfillment of which can only be deferred at the risk of dangerous frustrations with irreparable consequences), all the while guaranteeing one's partner immediate compensation (if women give themselves for money, it is because they do not give themselves for nothing). Venality is a form of refusal of offering a gift, of one's gratuity. It enables sexual fulfillment and the negation of an amorous exchange. It is in this sense that the theme of venal sexuality appears also to be inscribed in the general movement of interpersonal disintegration.

Danger!

The consequences of this type of behavior are that one's sexual partner is in fact quite often a stranger, and this is ultimately rather risky. It is here that another important theme in the representation of sexual activity in the synopses comes into play: sex is extremely dangerous. More often than not it leads characters toward death rather than toward life. At best, the strangers whom they encounter in the street transmit diseases to them; at worst there are knifings, razor slashes, strangling, poisoning, murder, they set fire to their houses, open up the gas lines. On the middle ground: they take their photos, blackmail them, implicate them in murders, steal their clothes, their money, even their souls and their youth.

Les petites annonces

A woman in a tight-fitting dress is seated at the terrace of a café. A man holding a newspaper arrives and sits at her table without hesitation. The woman looks at him coldly. He shows her the ad. The woman removes her hood and frees her red hair while asking him if he likes the color. The man compliments her and asks why she answered the ad. For your death, she replies.

The man, surprised, laughs without understanding.

The woman looks at him right in the eyes and tells him that she always destroys the pride of a man she desires. Intrigued and relieved, the man jokes around while putting

out his cigarette. The woman relaxes and teases him, sensu-
alizes the conversation.

[He follows her; she will take him to an almost empty
loft, get him drunk on vodka, and with her father's help
poison him and get rid of the body.] The next day in another
café the woman sits down at a table and opens a newspaper.

One encounters exactly the same type of danger in dating
services, ads in the *Chasseur français*,[5] meetings through the
Internet, women who come to see you in prison or even, quite
simply, in encounters at the bistro:

Lili

This is a tale written in the first-person singular: a young woman meets
a bookseller in a café. They talk. She tells him, "while using an imaginary heroine," the story of her life: all those murders committed by
a girl who had been raped, who can no longer stand for a man to
touch her, who lives with the horror of the crimes that she commits
in spite of herself. A romance develops. They talk. Exchanges. Hope.
He leads her away, talks to her softly; tries to convince her, to calm
her, tells her she is cured, that he loves her, that happiness exists. "I
believed it for a minute. Until the moment when I noticed the knife.
I killed him, knowing that that wound engraved in me would never
disappear."

It is not surprising that violence and sex are associated in
this way insofar as most of the plots follow criminal story lines.
It is therefore the genre chosen that imposes this type of unfolding. Since, moreover, the texts tell few stories of passion, the
crime of passion is rarely found in the synopses. It is therefore
perfectly logical, since there have to be assassinations, that it is
strangers who carry out the crimes.

5. *Le chasseur français* is a French monthly magazine devoted to hunting and
fishing. It has been published since 1885 and has a circulation of six hundred thousand. Its section on marriage announcements is particularly well known; it is a common subject of many jokes.

Suspicions . . .

Readers are quite aware of that fact. But it also happens that other characters suspect as much. In a certain number of tales, the dramatic impetus of the story rests on the moment when the main character becomes aware of the perilous nature of his or her situation: like a chemical reaction, the amorous escapade then veers from pleasure to anguish. Rightly or wrongly.

Roberto, Roberto, mon amour, ou le portefeuille imitation écaille

In a lovely apartment on rue Vaneau, Hannah, an attractive thirty-five-year-old woman, says goodbye to her husband and two children. She appears feverish and agitated. She is leaving for a few days with a little suitcase that holds the novel she is completing. In fact, she is going to meet a man. "They've known each other for hardly a month. They always meet in a certain cafe. They know very little about each other." He appears very much in love. He makes many plans. She seems much more reserved, hesitant. They get into a car. The suburbs fly by. They arrive at a small house, a little run-down, "which stinks of mediocrity." They settle in, he goes out to do some shopping and returns with his arms full of gifts. He then pulls her toward him onto the bed, softly, but when he tells her that he wants to have a child with her, "she realizes that she has put herself in an impossible mess. She refuses to make love. Later, when she wakes up she is surprised to find she is alone. Quickly, she gathers up her things and hurries to the door. It is dead-bolted. Her escapade turns into a nightmare. She thinks of the number of women who disappear each year in France. She believes she is being held hostage in this suburban house. She left without leaving an address and no one in the world has any idea where she is right now. (. . .) More dead than alive, she is terrified to realize that she knows nothing about Roberto.

The sexual activity presented is so often deadly that we are surprised to discover it can also open up onto life:

Le business d'Harmonie

This shy young woman, around thirty years old, with an average figure and mediocre appearance, works at Center 329 of the Department of Social Security. She didn't win the TV contest, "Happiness at Your Doorstep." The slice of veal liver she had prepared did not inspire her partner. She nevertheless wins a consolation prize: a wonderful week in Tunisia at the vacation resort El Ashour. Obviously, nothing happens as planned: in the airplane, as the only woman without a companion, she is watched by all the passengers. She arrives in suffocating heat, her suitcase is too heavy, her dress too short, men undress her with their eyes, she blushes. She arrives "in a tourist complex that shines brilliantly in the starry night like a big fat birthday cake." There is a young waiter in the hotel. She decides to seduce him, awkwardly, with a little money and much too much emotion. Neither one of them really knows how to go about it. Neither one of them really knows what they are looking for. A not very romantic adventure then follows that is not at all what she dreamed of.

In the last scene: she is back at home, in Paris, in her kitchen, she is watching "Happiness at Your Doorstep" on TV. She gets up. We then see by her rounded stomach that she is pregnant.

In all of the synopses we are struck by the degree to which sex is present but eroticism absent. In a general way, the sensibility of the texts is not at all hedonistic. Has the sexual revolution played itself out on a background of sexual violence and amorous misery? In reality, there is something that leads us to temper this impression: a recurring reference to the sensuality of women.

THE RHETORIC OF FEELINGS

The classic fictional scenario of thwarted love, which has fed a huge amount of literature throughout the centuries, from *Tristan and Yseult* to *West Side Story*, including *Romeo and Juliet* and *Paul et Virginie*, is conspicuously absent in our screenplays. In traditional societies where each person, from the richest of princes to the most humble of artisans, lived through the support of their patrimony, the marriage union was much too serious an issue to be left to the amorous whimsy of young people. Various means were thus used to control their excesses. It was within this context that the rhetoric of passion blossomed and spread. Contemporary societies have broken those restraints. Has the lifting of social constraints and moral taboos brought about the death of passion?

In any event, in our synopses, this type of passionate language is found only in very specific circumstances. First, in those that are anchored in the past: amorous passion thrives in works of historical fiction—this begins with ancient Gaul and ends in the 1960s. At that point a certain discretion appears to have been imposed: is it linked to the weakening of the passionate feeling itself, or does it instead come out of a new form of modesty? It is as if the standards of indecency have shifted and the current norms, which more easily authorize demonstrations of sexuality, have made the expression of passion an indecent exhibition. When the body is unclothed, the heart is masked. There is then always something to hide.

La légende de l'homme de boue

A journalist and his assistant are on the lookout for a story about a small village located on the Gironde estuary. He makes a few disillusioned remarks about his assignment: the never-ending banal chronicle of a place where nothing happens. She then suggests that he inquire into a legend buried in the most ancient memories of the locale and have it played out by the inhabitants of the village. It is the story of the impossible love of a young noblewoman, Elise, and a handsome fisherman, Fabien, who ultimately died, covered with mud, in the swamps. In the course of the filming the villagers remember a statue, the work of a local artist, that is buried in the hay in an old barn. It is dug out: it portrays Fabien; the eyes are in perfect condition, shocking in their realism, magnetic. The journalist and his assistant are overwhelmed. They snap out of it through a joke:

HE: What a joke. Nobody tells stories like that anymore. It makes me think of *Les visiteurs du soir*.

SHE: A real tearjerker—those kind of films don't work any
more.

HE: In a certain way, it is the approach that needs another
go-round. I'm going to go over the script. As its title:
Sucker? What do you think?

Tales of amorous passion also occur elsewhere, far, far
away. Several synopses, whose authors come from other lands,
lead us into such universes: the rhetoric of passion has become
very exotic.

Bala ani Sôna

The story takes place in an African village. "Bala is mesmerized by
the luminous beauty of Sôna. He dreams of making her his wife; she
is henceforth the single object of his love." But she is promised to
another. "Bala, distraught, wanders through the village thinking only
of his beloved. Every night the lovers meet and lavish each other
with poetic images to express their love for each other." On either
side of the wall where the young girl is held prisoner they live the
fatality of their love. Then they flee. The young man is bitten by a
snake. "He dies, leaving his love alone, condemned to wander forever in the mountains."

In our land, in our time, among our contemporaries, truly
monumental obstacles are required for a man and a woman to
give free rein to the expression of a true passion.

Embrasse-moi

This is a situation that might occur when a boy falls madly in love
with an extraterrestrial full of marvelous talents who has come to our
planet with the single aim of getting pregnant in order to repopulate
her own planet, which has been devastated by a natural disaster.
"The separation is inevitable. The two lovers drown in each other's
eyes." She reembarks for her distant destination, bringing both her
baby and a basket filled with earthly fruits and vegetables.

Coming from another planet favors the blossoming of blind
love. Coming from another place in time isn't bad, either.

Les anachroniques

Two noblemen from the ancien régime land in our era in an attempt to aid their king, whose life is threatened. They appear in a field and enter a small village near Paris, where they are taken for revelers from a costume ball. They quench their thirst with a glass of red wine for which they pay with a few golden louis. One of them falls in love with a young journalist, Claire Mantel, who introduces him to modern life. When it comes time for him to leave, she tries to hold him back. "In the field that had first greeted him, Claire and Octave walk side by side in silence, their hearts beating furiously. Finally she says to him: 'If you leave, you will die, you will have your head cut off.' 'So it is written.' he fatalistically replies. She has already tried a thousand times before, but she tries again. A thousand times he has said no, and has shaken his head. He cries out that he will write to her. An amused response is lost in the icy air. She is alone. Gone, the two friends are saluted by the cry of crows." A few years later, accompanied by the conservator, she consults the archives in the chateau of the Brandeban family. She discovers letters written by an original ancestor addressed to a certain Claire Mantel of 1991. The last letter was dated June 12, 1792.

But even in these Draconian conditions, things do not always work out. In *Le portrait*, a young man has fallen in love with a woman from the eighteenth century whose face he has seen in a painting. He builds a time machine in an attempt to go back and meet her. Unfortunately, he never manages to regulate his machine precisely, and he arrives either too early (the beauty is still only a baby) or too late (she is already an old woman).

The theme of time travel is used often.[6] This is most likely

---

6. Here is another example of similarity without previous influence. Six synopses portray time travel. This was before the film *Les visiteurs* came out (*Les visiteurs*, a film by Jean Marie Poiré, came out in 1993 and was a huge success in France. It tells the story of a medieval knight, the count de Montmirail, who along with his valet Jacquouille La Fripouille, as the result of the mistake of a magician, lands right in the middle of the twentieth century, and who discovers all the transformations that have affected his land and his descendants). This situation recurred very often. During the telephone conversations I had with the authors, we often commented on the phenomenon. ("And yet I had written the text before the film came out." "But, I know very well. I read it, I was just as surprised as you were." "Good. Then it's popular").

because it is a narrative device that enables an author to bring the past to the present through artificial means and therefore to overcome the feeling of disconnection that characterizes a relationship with the past. But it is also a way to deal with certain themes that are considered unapproachable in the current time.

Love, All the Same

There is something very strange in all of this. Is it truly possible that in one generation we have thus obliterated what seemed to be one of the most interesting dimensions of the human adventure? And what if it were I who understood nothing? I reviewed the texts again. It was then that they began to take on a different meaning. I saw two bodies of work defined where in the beginning I had noticed only one. The first was composed of synopses written by authors over thirty-five, the second by younger authors. It was primarily the first group that was characterized by an exile of passion and difficulties in relationships. The second group had a different tone, which was, in fact, more allusive; one had to read between the lines. It was not necessarily an amorous sentiment that was missing, but rather its expression, as if to inscribe it in words would appear incongruous, ridiculous, or not very reasonable. I kept thinking about the recurring reference to the notion that women are beautiful and sensual. I kept thinking about what I had noticed in the texts concerning music. Sensuality, music. A good way to short-circuit language. What if our authors were simply suspicious of words?

And suddenly I saw a huge number of love stories blossoming in the material. Very discreet. They never evolved within romantic excess. And above all such stories were associated with two ages in life: youth and old age. And in between, there was an intermission of some fifty years or so.

Mobile Love

The love stories deal with postadolescence (fifteen- to twenty-five-year-olds) and are always found within networks of friends.

They are not stories of one single couple, but always intercon-
nected stories of several couples, couples that are formed, break
apart; "I love you, I don't love you anymore," couples that are
discussed among girlfriends ("and he told me that he had told
you that he had told her"), that connect friends, lovers, a future
friend, an ex-lover, a future lover, an ex-friend, etc. It is very
complicated, but rather nice. Often a text begins with the usual
introduction of the main characters: Laure, Eric, Christine, and
Gérard; Béatrice, Clara, Jacques, and Grégoire; etc. A few physical characteristics for each personage (for more specifics one
has to wait for casting), a few psychological elements, a little
biographical information are briefly sketched.

And the great plot can begin.

J'ai sorti mon chien du congélateur

The atmosphere grows increasingly tense: Caroline, sarcas-
tic, upsets everyone. Fred finally kicks her out, much to
Gloria's delight. Nico is uneasy, but stays all the same. They
are at Manu's. Fred finally decides to call Virginie.

[Then:] Nico is sad. Caroline is really mad. Someone arrives, Fred hopes it's Virginie, but it's only Benoît, who has
come to show them the final poster. It's love at first sight
between him and Gloria.

Breakups, dramas, jealousies (thirty-year-old women vs.
twenty-year-old girls), feigned unawareness, revenge, decep-
tion. Everything might end with threesomes, girls who go from
boy to boy, boys who share a woman they have all slept with.

Thérèse et les transports en commun

To impress her, Eric, the naive young neighbor, has the
idea one day of introducing her to his childhood friend, Fabrice, a dashing jack-of-all-trades who immediately seduces
Thérèse—and her friend Catherine.

Eric desperately tries to channel the storm he has un-
leashed. His strategy consists of putting Catherine into the

arms of Fabrice, in order to keep Thérèse for himself. But he wasn't counting on Fabrice, who had certainly seen that both girls liked him—or on Thérèse, who does not let go easily.

An amiable settling of accounts between the two boys. They divide up the girls just about equally—except that both of them want Thérèse—and Fabrice wants Catherine, too!

The settling ends in a fight. Fortunately interrupted by the memory of their friendship. OK. Eric can have Thérèse, and Catherine will go with Fabrice.

But they were forgetting about the girls!

Amorous wandering has a consequence: every relationship is marked by those that preceded it. In abandoning the rhetoric of passion, lovers have also abandoned the hope for eternity that was associated with it: a liaison takes its place in an environment marked by the alternation of fission and fusion of amorous molecules, within a group of one's peers.

L'amour en quatre

ERIK: How long did you live with him?
ANNE: Five years.
ERIK: That's a long time. You kicked him out?
ANNE: He left on his own.
ERIK: Why?
ANNE: Do I ask you so many questions?
ERIK: No, because you don't give a damn.
ANNE: You're right.
ERIK: I love your candor, my love.
ANNE: If you don't like it, you can leave.

Historians have shown how traditional societies were cautious of love, the violent and uncontrollable irruption of which threatened the complex edifice of matrimonial strategies. While reading all these texts one wonders whether we are not once again in a culture where feeling is viewed as dangerous, no longer for the entire group, but for the subject, him or herself.

Les rêves en miettes

You're twenty years old and have all your teeth, and then Bam! love gives you an uppercut in your jaw. For Nadine, it is an actor, Gérard, a swaggerer whom she meets on the set of a mediocre film in which she's making her debut as an actress. Gérard seduces everyone, including Nadine, of course, who is so lit up by this belated first amorous experience that she is already dreaming of marriage. Don't forget the parents, since Gérard is ambitious: he wants to open up a bistro on the coast with his friends. In the end, the only person this pompous Gérard leaves cold is Patrick, Philippe's best friend. Because he is in love with Nadine!

You're twenty-years-old and have all your dreams and then, Pow! love sends you an uppercut right in your heart. And a slap, as well! Philippe, an intern in a large radio station, falls in love with Carole, makes the mistake of taking her to dinner in a bar frequented by prostitutes, promises her, under the influence of alcohol, a role in a radio series that doesn't exist, in short—everything goes sour! Carole classifies him in the category of the fake-o/snoboids and turns a deaf ear to his desperate advances. Philippe can only write his masterpiece now, or risk never seeing her again.

We should point out that marriage is once again on young couples' horizons: the idea of marriage is sometimes brought up. It is as if that institution were the object of a sort of symbolic reinvestment: it has not, for all that, lost its precariousness, but it is once again filled with meaning. This does not imply, of course, a simple return to a traditional form of marriage. After the feminist and militant battle of the seventies against a marriage to be destroyed, after the peaceful cohabitation of the eighties in the face of a devalued marriage, there comes a new state of mind. As if the promise of marriage once again belonged to the amorous lexicon: it is a way of indicating a difference between earlier unions, a way of expressing a hierarchy in successive amorous adventures.[7]

It is no doubt for that reason that it is so intolerable to former partners: several stories are based on rather similar plots. A girl or a boy receives an announcement informing them of the coming marriage of a former partner. They immediately go into action and do everything in their power to make the union fail. Out of pure cynicism, defiance, or despair. All the same, marriage does not mark a definitive and irrevocable exit out of amorous wandering: "The day of her marriage Thérèse notices an attractive man among the guests. The adventure isn't over— as long as there are men!"

TRANSITORY NETWORKS

In these synopses love stories are found within the networks of a youthful sociability: they are woven from a thick interpersonal skein, and this is precisely what distinguishes them from the novelistic scenarios of romantic love that place a man and a woman alone, face to face.

And it would seem that this intertwining, at a given age, of ties of friendship and ties of love is translated by a sort of contamination of one bond by the other. In *L'amitié*, Francesco Alberoni scrutinizes a sort of anatomy of feelings in order to uncover the specificities of love and friendship.[8] In rereading this work, one is struck by the increased blending of the two types of bonds in the universe of the synopses, at least in the modes of their expression: it appears that amorous wandering

---

7. This state of mind accompanied an evolution in practices, since the number of marriages fell in considerable proportions; we went from 412,000 marriages in 1976 to 265,000 in 1987. In five years the decline has been halted; the slight shuddering that seems to indicate the beginning of an increase must not cause any illusions; the number has stabilized at an extremely low level, so that, if current tendencies continue, half of an age group will ultimately remain single.

8. Francesco Alberoni, *L'amitié* (Paris, 1985).

adopts a vocabulary that is much closer to one of friendship than to one of passion.

These texts therefore also portray the models of sociability of a generation of characters. We see the formation of solid friendships, with their specific rituals: going out together to bars, meeting in bistros, parties.

La vie en HLM

Everyone goes to the birthday party at Karim's house. (. . .) In the kitchen three girls are fixing snacks, singing. A chubby young man nibbles from the trays. Others decide to go to the cafe to get some ice. In the living room a young man with dreadlocks is carefully preparing joints and puts them in jars. A group forms to play chess, others start dancing to rap music. The light is filtered. Couples form and dance a slow dance. Others are sitting on the ground leaning on sofa cushions, playing cards, eating, drinking whisky or passing around a joint.

Very little is eaten in the synopses: characters smoke a lot, drink vast quantities, much more than their thirst requires, but conviviality is never associated with sharing a meal. Often relationships are formed around shared artistic ambitions: plays produced together ("to give a show for free for the folks in the neighborhood who never go to the theater"), but especially music. Indeed, music appears as the primary means of unification in these informal groups. Jazz, rock, rap, or even classical music. It is both an opportunity to meet and also the single structuring mode of planned sociability. For on the whole, the sociability described in the synopses is very unstructured: it is not inscribed within the framework of a community organization. There are no political parties, no sports associations, no religious communities, no gangs, no clubs: never any form of instituted or institutionalized relationships. Social exchanges are not inscribed in an environment that frames relationships and guarantees their endurance. There is no solidarity connected to a slightly formalized community with its pacts, its lasting debts, its rituals, its contracts (except for a few suburban gangs).

This situation is clearly not fortuitous: it reflects an irrepressible distrust of all instituted structure, which is seen as the agent, with its codes and rules, for the perils of a fascistic drift. And it is surely not by chance that the few organizations described are always malevolent and pernicious associations.

However, these friendships between pals are threatened by terrible centrifugal forces, and many of the texts tell of the bursting apart of social networks: there is professional or amorous competition, money problems, residential mobility, or the success of one of the members in a group artistic project—all of these factors can contribute to breaking up the group.

IMPROBABLE FRIENDSHIPS

Only the friendship between people who are considered opposites can endure: we see differences in social status, in personalities, but above all in age, the favorite relationship being that which joins the young child and the elderly person. The insistence with which the authors note the differences between the protagonists is such that it cannot be fortuitous: it is clearly *because* this form of friendship connects characters who have characteristics that are defined as antinomic that it is presented as being possible. We see once again what we have already seen on several occasions: it is similarities, unclear definitions, the confusion of status and roles, that lead to difficulties in relationships.

Here are a few examples of such disparate relationships: a famous Hollywood actress and a prostitute from the slums of Los Angeles; a little child and a puppeteer; a seven-year-old orphan and an old witch in the mountains; a twenty-year-old burglar and an old Italian man who is dying in his hospital bed and wants, before he dies, to be blessed by a priest in his cassock; a distinguished provincial grandmother and a young Moroccan delinquent; a burglar and an old news vendor; a teddy boy on the lam and a young rock musician; a down-and-out young woman and a film star who meet in the same hospital room after they both attempted suicide; a little Asian boy and a very old woman; an eight-year-old child and an old bird-catcher; a twenty-five-year-old screenwriter and an eighty-year-old man who escaped from a hospice; a woman cop and a North African woman; an Italian child and a blind woman; a little boy and a department store Santa Claus; a dynamic young executive and a bum named Philémon who brings the professional man with him to sleep under the bridges, etc.

Through a curious inversion, whereas couples are formed within groups, these friendships are relationships that involve just two people. They never metamorphose into amorous relationships, at the risk of being condemned. These friendships bring support, warmth, and comfort only because they escape the climate of backbiting and generalized competition. But at the same time they are such improbable relationships that one cannot be sure that they escape the general feeling of the rise of solitudes.

Four

Solitudes

Sale temps pour les pigeons

Lousy Weather for Pigeons is primarily the story of a man who could have been, who should have been something other than the delivery man for Legros-Fils franchises, but who, as he himself says, must have missed a fork in the road somewhere in his adolescence. He is a thirty-year-old man who hides a secret wound that makes him an apathetic figure who believes in nothing, especially not in himself, and shows, if not scorn, at least no confidence in humanity, indeed, a certain disgust, in any event, indifference. He does his work without conviction, visits no one, lives alone. He, himself, doesn't really know what he expects from life. Undoubtedly nothing.

[He will suddenly fall in love and experience a true passion for a woman, while a series of murders crashes in on their surroundings. He doesn't trust her. He thinks she is guilty. Yet he doesn't give up on the relationship, all the while knowing he will doubtless be the next victim. He goes out of his house; the hand of a killer strikes him. It wasn't she . . .]

But Luc cried out her name. And they understand at that moment—she, that he had always suspected her, and he, that he has just lost her. Each one will return to their solitude. A solitude that in truth they had never really left.

Here, now, is the final scene. The individual finds himself once again face to face with himself. We have left the universe of social representations, characterized by those highly stereo-typed emblematic figures. We have also left the universe of psychological relationships, with its interpersonal difficulties. Everything now revolves around a single character. The camera focuses very tightly on a face. The background, always the same, is only sketched. And yet, in this final stage, the same situation occurs: this time it is the tie that connects the character to his own past, the bond that connects him to the place where he used to live, the very bond that "holds him together," that also comes undone.

This section will be presented much more briefly, although it groups some hundred texts, quite simply because these synopses are not very easy to summarize: they do not really tell a story, but search rather to evoke atmospheres. They are often written in a more literary style than the others and resemble short stories more than they do screenplays.

Following a car accident:

La mésange et le hérisson

Sand, railing, rows of grating, I picked up everything! A taste of blood in my throat, a taste of warm blood with the familiar bitterness. To think that I can't stand blood sausage! Smoke in pastel hues dripped down from the sky. No suffering, the shock had numbed me pretty much. The front half of the car had one of those looks: the left tire had literally flown off and was sitting on what remained of the hood like a figurine on top of a layer cake. I was unable to move at all. Someone spoke to me, I answered, so I was OK! After a quick maneuver with a can opener, I was removed from the cake.

From the ceiling of the ambulance there flowed a blue tenderness in heavy and warm drops; Ingrid's concerned face had something abstract about it. Her icy hand breathed on my forehead like a parenthesis opening and closing.

"You'll come and see me, right?"

On my hospital bed, a strangely swaddled puppet, hanging by its strings, looked at me with a sly expression. The evasiveness of hours, the lethargy of time exasperated me. Held by unfriendly bonds, I had no other distraction than the succession of routine visits and no other themes of discussion than the reiterated narration of my luge party.

Ingrid was kept waiting!

What was going on?

So many hours, so many people, so many pills, so many looks at my watch, so many forced smiles, so many unanswered questions have torn the pages of a motionless calendar.

Un fusil et des bonbons

A sunny and cold autumn morning, the paths in a cemetery in a small town. Franck Fonhesterazi, sixty-two, short and out of shape, an employee in the stockroom of the small post office, buries his parents, with whom until that day he had lived in a small house. (. . .)

A few days later, after thirty years of good and loyal service, Franck Fonhesterazi retires and receives as a farewell gift from the government ministry the four volumes of the Folio edition of *A la recherche du temps perdu* by Marcel Proust. On the job he had made neither friends or enemies. He worked alone. He was so quiet that his departure goes completely unnoticed.

Following that, Franck Fonhesterazi puts the little family house that he can no longer keep up for sale. It is sold very quickly to a real estate investor who is going to tear down the house to build a large apartment building in its place. Franck Fonhesterazi then moves to a small two-room lodging in the Bleuets complex that is on the edge of town and whose proximity to the old-age club has attracted a large number of retirees. Upon his arrival at the Bleuets everyone greets the new neighbor with curiosity. At the beginning Franck Fonhesterazi does not respond. He isn't happy in this complex, he refuses to participate in any of the activities in the building. He continues to frequent the places of his earlier life. A diabetic, he obtains his insulin from the pharmacy close to the little house where he lived with his parents. Every day at noon he goes to get a portion of the daily special at the deli across from the post office where he no longer works. One day he goes in the post office and instead of being greeted as is fitting for someone who spent thirty years of his life there, he is taken for a mere client and asked what he wants, and without answering, he leaves the building.

In the background, like figures in Chinese shadow theater, we find characters and elements that we already know; the developer, the club for dynamic retirees, but the accent is placed on the main character and his solitude. Sometimes the break with the past goes as far as amnesia. The main character no longer knows who he is, where he comes from, where he is going. He remembers neither his name nor his age, but since he is of interest to no one, this lost identity does not represent a dramatic element. The screenplay mixes flashbacks with close-ups. In public parks. Subway stations. Airports.

WANDERING

For characters do not just break with their past; they also often abandon the place where they used to live. One day a man leaves his job, his wife, his family, his life, leaves behind him an entire completed part of his existence and goes in search of himself. All the texts describe this process in the same way: it does not involve a maturely pondered decision, but rather a sudden, irresistible, irreversible impulse. In general, the character doesn't know the motives for his action. "Then without knowing why, Dubois leaves his city. He walks without turning around, leaving his little life behind him. It is Christmas night in Issoire, as in other cities. On the road that leads to the edge of town a man is walking followed by his dog. He must be forty, maybe older. Maybe younger. Not young or old, one of those faces you forget right after you see it. Sadness sticks to his features like a light burden that deadens his look. A little insidious and persistent pain. Like a stone in his shoe. He is wearing a Santa Claus costume" (*La vie petite*).

This wandering is fraught with encounters. Those encountered are also uprooted, and they are presented stripped-down: the one encountered is called the Other, the Stranger, the Man or the Woman: "It is noon. The sea is blue, the sky limitless. A very pale sky, slightly covered. There is a man who walks on the quay, a woman in the shadow of the houses." Or, on the contrary, they are characterized in a strange way, not always very evocative: "On his way he meets a dangerous post office employee who is carrying a large grocery bag, a Homeric homeless man who is pushing a ubiquitous supermarket cart, a nostalgic police commissioner, a painter in love with nocturnal birds." Or even "a crazy songwriter, an old priest stiff-jointed with wisdom and rheumatism, a taxi driver/writer/music lover, a female poet who cultivates blue tamarisks."

We are in any case poles apart from the descriptions of characters anchored more solidly in the social space: the wanderers are not conventionalized in a simple way, but are on the contrary qualified by a certain number of composite characteristics. In fact, they are representative of a break in all conventional forms that mirrors their wandering: the identity of the characters is defined by an association of unexpected details or attributes.

Similarly, dialogued scenes portray exchanges that have a disjointed and discontinuous form. Sometimes they occur entirely in an internal monologue. It even happens that every trace of communication disappears, and one no longer hears anything except the sound of the media in the background:

Jonas ou le tableau dans la jungle

Flames devour the spectators in a stadium while the Nazi torturers are reborn through the fault of a goalie: the bodies of Timisoara are exhumed and the complementary number is thirteen. Impossible to escape the din of the bombs, during this time charming white globules calmly devour dirty germs, Rocky knocks out the evil Soviet Goliath, but hands off my buddy, we'll take care of it. A little girl drowns before our hungry television eyes. My God, lively Hunger dear Patrick Sabatier luckily OMO washes whiter and Master Gillot-Pétré has placed his yellow pouch, bombs fall on a city, on a mother and her child . . .

Jonas is informed, reassured not to receive that bomb, but what color should he paint his sky? What is he going to paint on this canvas?

THE FRAGMENTED SUBJECT

The final stage is the subject's break with himself. The individual is split into multiple personalities. This can provide a thematic plot for police films: an administrator of justice in search of a murderer in fact discovers he is the assassin he is hunting down; every day a man receives death threats on his answering machine that he has been sending himself from the phone booth in front of his building and ends up dying "the final victim of his own personality." This theme can also sometimes inspire comedies (a young detective is capable of instantly adopting the personality of the different people he is looking for). It also forms the pretext for psychological dramas. The character then seems to divide himself through scissiparity. The simplest version is the one where he harbors two beings in himself.

L'homme sans frontière

Vincent Delvent divides himself between two lives: he has a house on both sides of the border, and "he gets on the road, endless comings and goings between each half of himself. These trips on D419, the departmental road of great treachery, as he calls it, brings an atmosphere and a music that will give rhythm to the sequences of the film. The light must support this principle, favor the mystery by creating a sort of poetry. In the mist of this long journey, Vincent Delvent searches for the meaning of his own story."

But sometimes there is much more. A young woman changes her personality each time she changes her look. She ends up *parasitized* by the characters she has copied. A man who goes in search of the woman whom he loved when he was an adolescent has difficulty finding her: in each place where she has spent time she was functioning with a different personality.

And a certain number of texts are entirely devoted to the inner dialogue that is carried on between the various parts of a divided subject.

Le feu sacré

Victor has arrived in a barren place, a sort of uncultivated field. The night is an opaque black. The wind and thunder have a dull sound. The street seems far away, as do the lights of the city. He turns around, hesitates, looks for his path, but at the moment when he wants to leave, a huge bolt of lightning startles him. The crack of the thunder covers his cry. He falls to the ground.

Calm having returned, we see his stretched-out body on the ground. A gentle wind. Soft crackling and semidarkness. Slight lateral movement toward a small, intimate, and contained fire around which four men are seated. They watch the fire in silence, pensive and concerned at the same time. These four men resemble each other, but they all have their own unique look.

"The yuppie" is preoccupied. (. . .) He is distinguished, slightly fine-featured, dressed in a conservative and elegant fashion (dark suit, tie), impeccable in casual refinement. He seems full of method and organization. His attaché case sits in front of him.

"The slang man" looks like a biker, tattooed, like a rock star. Blouson jacket, T-shirt, jeans, sandals, and cap. He is stretched out on his side, nonchalant, smoking a fluorescent joint whose smoke rings break apart, and makes noises like "bof," "pff," "yeah," "ah!" skeptical and disillusioned. (. . .)

"The mystic" is dressed all in white, a full tunic and wide pants, barefoot with a shaved head. He keeps his eyes shut, sits cross-legged and concentrates on breathing deeply. (. . .)

"The artistic one" with the "cool look," a black pullover, dark glasses and ponytail, wild pants of a clothing designer, sketches broad strokes on a roll of dark but transparent paper. (. . .)

These four characters live in Victor and form his personality. They have the moral responsibility for the one they call "Our Dear Person." However, they are all quite stubborn. Each one of them wants to dominate the others and to take power by imposing his tastes and his way of life. Their conflicts and their disagreements are reflected in Victor, who has moods, doubts, and anger. (. . .) This story tells how difficult it is to get along well with yourself by showing how difficult it is to get along well with others.

This is not a portrayal that piles up the different versions of the self and exhibits their potential conflicts. The representation of the subject is not the vertical image of a geological superposition of successive layers; rather it is horizontal and sequential. That is, a subject's interiority is not made up of organized elements following a single ordering principle, but rather of fragments juxtaposed alongside each other. Out of this, the different aspects of a personality arise successively without the individual being able to place them in a hierarchy or to choose in order to know which one is the best, the most desirable, or the most authentic. The subject is as if passively inhabited by different versions of himself and subject to their irruption.

The fragmentation of the subject is heavy with significance. In her article, Mary Douglas questions the meaning of the "unitary self" in which she sees the foundation of order in Western societies.

> Our civilization was founded on the rejection of the idea of the multiple "self," that is, of a "self" formed of several distinct "selves" that dominate different zones of choice and responsibility. We also reject the notion of a "passive self," whose actions are under the control of external forces, such as furies, gods, demons, or witches. Finally, the notion of a nonrational and arbitrary "self" is also rejected. In fact, these notions have been re-

jected for reasons of judicial order: because we needed a "united self" to establish the notion of responsibility. Other civilizations prosper while having quite different conceptions of the "self." Other theories of the "self" are unacceptable to us, for we wish to insist on complete responsibility. Each time we place blame, insisting on complete responsibility, we reinforce the idea of a unified "self." Each time we pardon, we render more acceptable the idea of a "passive self" or of a "multiple self." The idea of a multiple "self" enables sweet pardons like polished fictions.[1]

We can indeed see what this idea might bring to an understanding of all the texts. We began with the idea of the crisis of institutions and by measuring the consequences of that crisis. We find ourselves again with the idea of a weakening of the notion of responsibility. A new step is taken: every form of order imposed from outside is considered to be an unbearable strike against individual freedom. But we cannot substitute an internal order for it, because the individual himself is fragmented and therefore in part irresponsible. There are therefore two complementary issues at hand. We measure the consequences of this situation: without order imposed from outside and without adherence to a personal ethics of individual responsibility, how can society be made to function?

It is possible to go farther with regard to interpersonal relationships and look at the issue that has concerned us since the beginning, the question of bonds. Mary Douglas's article focuses on judicial responsibility and therefore concerns the social dimension of the individual. One can also be more specifically concerned with an individual's interpersonal dimension. It is indeed possible that by accepting this idea of the "self" divided into "a committee of quasi people," one in fact renders all relationships impossible.

The individual lacks too many certainties about himself to be able to undertake a commitment. He has chosen to surrender his life to the logic of his feelings. He is subject to their variations, for feelings are supposed to vary. He can therefore

1. Mary Douglas, "La connaissance de soi," *Revue du Mauss* 8 (1990).

not take the risk of a commitment: he is too unstable to allow someone to depend on him. And he cannot take the risk of depending on anyone else, because the other is also changing. But then, in this climate of instability, what will become of the bond? For can a bond ever truly exist without dependency? And how can one live happily without ties?

We are in a situation that is different from the one we encountered regarding the increased number of unmarried couples.[2] At the time when the institution of marriage began to be challenged, young couples were defending militant positions: they wanted to establish their union only on feeling and rose up against the institution in the name of love. One has the impression that in the universe of the synopses this period has passed. Another stage has been reached, as if the characters have integrated the idea that feelings do not last. The issue they must henceforth resolve is rather this: how to enjoy others without taking the risk of depending on them, or—which amounts to the same thing—how can you preserve yourself in a situation of instability? These questions open up onto that reciprocal agreement on a weak commitment, in an economy of emotions in which each person seeks first to protect him- or herself. Out of this come that minimum sharing and the exile of passion, and regulation through money, the duty of egotism, and the complications that result from it.

There is, in fact, a difference between the texts studied in this third section and the other texts in the corpus. They bring to light an obvious dissymmetry: throughout the material the characters described are dominated by strategic ways of behaving. But when it is the subject himself who is at the center of the action, he is no longer cynical: he is disjointed. If the por-

2. I began my research on this subject studying the social changes in a Paris neighborhood in 1978, within the framework of the Action Thématique Programmée, CNRS Continuous Observation of Social and Cultural Change. I had then had the feeling that challenging the matrimonial institution formed a major evolution in the family and social structures that were thus being sketched surreptitiously. Cf. Sabine Chalvon-Demersay, "Les concubins du XIVème," Thèse de Troisième Cycle under the direction of Henri Mendras, Paris FNSP, 1981, and by the same author, *Concubin, concubine* (Paris, 1984).

trayals are internally coherent, there must be a way to go from that "doubt about oneself" to that "suspicion of the other."

In fact, it is possible to achieve this by resorting to the notion of *rational anticipation:* if the person standing in front of you is unpredictable, it is necessary to seek a way to render him more predictable. Fixing him in a negative position can constitute a response to this situation. Expecting the worst is of course a logical solution: it is both a way of avoiding the risks of disappointment and the best way to guard oneself against the dangers that the other presents. Thus the final link can be established, the one we lacked, between the movement of de-institutionalization, the absence of positivity, and the crisis of the bond. *Deinstitutionalization* brings about the instability that is accompanied by unpredictability. The consequence of this is the development of purely strategic representations that in turn brings about the disintegration of bonds. It is a bit complicated, but perfectly logical. The circle is closed. The film ends. Everything begins with the final image.

Conclusion

Stories and anecdotes have accumulated throughout the pages above. We have also gradually sketched a general tableau, the meaning of which we have finally been able to reveal. These thousand screenplay projects are remarkable in that they describe, in a coherent and precise manner, the nature of an impasse: the impossibility of contemporary society's bringing about any form of solidarity. The cause of this impasse, too, can be revealed: it is the desertion of institutions that degrades human relationships. This is what the scripts of the collection endlessly describe.

It is absolutely impossible to know whether the authors are aware of this. Only one thing can be asserted with confidence: their characters concretely experience the effects of that desertion in the form of a series of malaises. If we look again at three scenes that we have already viewed, we will see how the issues raised can always be understood as variations of this same difficulty.

On the stage of public life, the issue is raised by way of emblematic figures. Institutions are represented by characters. Their downfall is obvious: they are those cynical policemen, those tired teachers, those depressed social workers, those unhappy priests, etc. They are not hostile, but powerless. And their lack of power leaves the way open for all those who have some knowledge, even just a little, to abuse the power that comes with it. On all levels of a society in which each person is increasingly dependent on others, the experts are necessarily manipulators or monopolizers.

On the stage of intimacies, the family as an institution has come apart, and we must assess the consequences of this. There is no longer any admissible principle of hierarchizing and ordering, whether based on age or gender. The traditional order was unjust. But the current situation opens onto a confusion that is a source of violence. The parents of young adults are in competition with their offspring, women are in competition with men, old people act like children, and children have the wisdom of the elderly. Added to the traditional rivalries on the familial stage are all those new forms that create a climate of defiance and competition, the ultimate aspect of the disorder being incestuous deviations. The result is an inability to create and maintain a relationship. The only viable relationships are those that connect the most distant generations (relationships between grandparents and grandchildren, couples with a large gap in their ages), enabling a slight diminishing of the general climate of competition that reigns in familial relationships.

On the last stage, that of intimate self-consciousness, it is the individual himself who no longer manages to keep himself together. He refuses to regulate his behavior in terms of an ethic created outside of him. But the interiority that he must use as a guide is not stable. His personality is unstable, variable, multiple. It is made up of a succession of unstable impressions and feelings. It is not organized along a simple hierarchizing principle that would enable it to order good, evil, the preferable, the desirable. The individual no longer has the means to hierarchize goals and ends. He is therefore endlessly forced to listen to himself to find a guide for his own actions. But since his personality is fluctuating, this attention to himself can swallow him up completely, to the detriment of any other form of bond: this is the narcissistic deviation.

From all of this we can reconstruct the entire edifice of the screenplays from the inside out, beginning with the subject. It is because the individual is no longer stabilized by an order that he experiences doubt about himself. It is because he experiences doubt about himself that he prefers to adopt a defiant attitude with regard to others (which protects him the most and enables him to limit risks). And it is because society is composed of "others" that society can experience no possible renovation. This construction explains the strange atmosphere that permeates the corpus, one that sometimes takes the form of humor, but often of blasé disillusionment, and that in any event always reflects an acceptance of a certain form of fatality. The twilight of good feelings. The eradication of indignation. The world is rotten, but we can't change anything. Bastards are bastards, but characters have the vague impression that if they were in their place they would act just like them. To take on a critical position, it would be necessary to have a place from which to start, to escape the instability, the relativism, to find somewhere in oneself the feeling that continuity and positivity can exist. And it is precisely that which is lacking.

Therefore, it is not because there is no longer any collective hope for renewal in the world of the synopses that the characters are morose. Rather, the opposite is true. It is because characters are filled with uncertainty about themselves that they are faced with a universe without hope. We see well how this position brings the individual and the collectivity into play: it does not start on high in order to go downhill. It starts from the individual subject and ends with the collective group.

We now have the last piece of the puzzle, which is also the one by which all of the screenplay representations become perfectly coherent. Indeed, we are in a system in which everything ends with the individual. And he is either socially determined (on the stage of social life), or unstable (on the stage of individual consciousness), or both at the same time (on the stage of intimacies). That is, in all cases, *the subject is devoid of a strong individual essence.* In other words, an entire building is being built upon a foundation that is crumbling.

Whether it is *because* the characters are subject to blind forces of social determinism, or *because* they are unstable and dependent on the movements of a fragmented interiority, it is impossible for them to act autonomously. It is the tension between these two extremes—the social and the personal—that is at the heart of the crisis that pervades the world of the screenplays: in both cases the characters are prisoners of situations that strip them of any possibility of taking hold of their lives.

It is here that we find the root of the malaise that pervades the synopses. But it is also here that the work of Charles Taylor, and in particular *The Ethics of Authenticity,* is extremely enlightening. Taylor enables us, in fact, to understand the corpus and, moreover, to recognize the components of the crisis that has come to be crystallized within the material.

Taylor analyzes three malaises of contemporary society: the rupture of traditional frameworks has been the opportunity to acquire a certain freedom, but it has been accompanied by a disenchantment linked to the feeling of having lost that which was once provided by an integration into a broader community; the development of instrumental reason, which is transformed into a simple instrument of utilitarian calculation, has enabled technological progress and a certain freedom with regard to the needs of subsistence, but it has led to an ignoring of ultimate ends and a preferential focusing only on means. Finally, the uniformization of ways of life is accompanied by a feeling of a loss of diversity. There exists a whole current of thought that universally condemns individualism by denouncing the pernicious consequences of it. Starting with the principle that individualism has engendered extreme narcissism, the cult of the self, relativism and subjectivism, it proposes rejecting individualism completely and seeks to establish solidarities on new foundations: this is the communitarian alternative. Compared to this, Taylor has an original perspective. He starts with the assumption that the rise of individualism is irreversible. He recognizes its faults, yet he believes that those faults are not inescapable logical consequences of individualism, but are instead deviations that, in truth, are contrary to its founding principles. Indeed, the problem comes from the fact that supporters of individualism are rabid relativists: they refuse to reason from a foundation of common values and cannot defend the idea that one way of life might be preferable to another. Taylor undertakes to show that those supporters in fact adhere to an ethics that is *an ethics of authenticity*. But the problem is that they do not dare to claim kinship with it. Individualism is incapable of appearing as a moral ideal of authenticity. It nevertheless comprises a certain imperative: individualism rests on the notion that it is preferable to cultivate one's originality or to act in conformity with what one feels, to be in sync with oneself, than merely to be a conformist, but it does not attempt to argue in this direction. If supporters of individualism agree to recognize that they adhere to a moral ideal of authenticity, they might escape narcissism. Indeed, in order to understand why he is truly "authentic," the individual necessarily needs others: only a comparison with others enables him to confirm the value and the specificity of his choices. The confrontation with alterity leads him, in fact, not only to validate but even to consolidate the hierarchies he has established, which are those he holds dear and which define him. It is therefore not *against* but *through* the social bond that the individual can realize himself: to distinguish essential differences from those that are secondary, differences that are worthy of true involvement from those that have no real importance. In this way the individual can escape from relativism, from fractioning, and restore a principle for action. From this Taylor settles down to the reformulation of a positive individualism, which would not only *not* be incompatible with, but would even require reference to, shared social values. It is easy to see what this approach provides: first, it shows the connection and the interdependence of individual, collective, and social spheres; then it shows that the malaises that affect those spheres are intimately connected; finally, by proposing an intervention in the very heart of the malaise-creating process, Taylor suggests that it might be possible to reverse its momentum.

This reading of Taylor's work opens up new perspectives on the world of the synopses. In fact, it proposes cognitive tools that enable us to leave aside the alternative that makes the universe of the screenplays unbearable. Indeed, throughout this study we have focused on the dominant idea that an impasse was created out of the relationship between the disappearance of old orders and the destruction of all forms of bonds. The weakening of traditional social structures was not interpreted as opening into chaos—which would have been a reactionary assessment—but as bringing about the destruction of bonds—which is perhaps ultimately worse. But what if the dilemma that has thus been imposed were a false dilemma? There is perhaps no reason for the rise in individualism to result in the indictment of all forms of solidarity. Why couldn't the relaxing of social structures be considered an advance of freedom? Why would individualism automatically bring about the destruction of all forms of bonds? It is because we have transformed into unshakable logical opponents propositions that are in truth perhaps not in contrast, and because at present we do not possess the necessary way of thinking that would enable us to refute those assertions. The social representations that float around in the public arena are like clothes that are too tight. They lead to a hardening of the way in which we view the alternatives, instead of a desire to loosen it up. And this is undoubtedly why the characters are so wary of words.

Everyone knows that happy people don't have a story, and that good literature isn't created with positive feelings. There is, however, in all of the texts we have been studying, something that goes beyond the conventional rules of fiction. The entire corpus is imbued with an extreme sense of pessimism. In whatever direction one turns there is an impasse. There is no longer any form of positiveness at work in this social world. Yet it is not because the authors are incapable of portraying heroes; there are many of them in the works of historical fiction. If they have chosen to exile all positive characters from the social sphere, and all positive feelings from the interpersonal sphere, it is because they think it is the only suitable way to speak about contemporary society. And therein lies the major contribution of this corpus: *however diverse the authors might be,* however diverse their intentions, the sources of their inspiration, and the subjects they have dealt with might be, there is a *true consensus* with respect to social and interpersonal ills and to the pessimism that results from them.

And it seems that this pessimism extends far beyond the limits of our material. It pervades a climate of opinion and a much more general atmosphere that form the current manifestations of a culture of crisis. After the great hopes for freedom of the seventies, the "cool and tanned" individualism of the eighties, there has followed a period of extreme doubt: individualism has assumed a somber face, one that no longer looks toward hedonism, but toward destruction of bonds, etc. The corpus constitutes a stage for the appearance of this pessimism, a particularly interesting stage because it is organized around the media. And it is quite possible that the media constitute the focal point for the crystallization and the hardening of this specific atmosphere of anxiety.

THE SPIRAL OF POWERLESSNESS

If the corpus is so dark, this is not because it is filled with violence—violence is commonplace; we are used to it. It is because the characters are plunged into a spiral of impotency: there is a sense that they have lost any possibility of controlling their own destinies. This sense pervades all the texts, in more sinister forms, as well as in comical situations and in stories full of humor.

Events unfold as if the characters involved no longer have any margin for maneuvering. They are caught in a triple trap. An *economic trap:* they are in a world that no longer integrates those who do not obey the rules of performance. This is what is told by all those slightly miserable heroes who are relegated to the margins of society and remain there without any hope of reintegration; they are in a society that refuses to look at issues in any other way than in terms of economics, whereas economic perspectives are destroying the society. A *sociological trap:*

characters are defined by their social status and imprisoned in
behaviors that that status dictates to them; their social position
is constantly converted into fatality. Their society offers absolutely no possibility for promotion, except through art or
through the lottery (and a few others forms of instant monetary
enrichment); society has become an implacable machine de-
signed to reproduce destinies, and each person is automatically
associated with the behaviors that his position imposes on him.
Victim or scoundrel, malevolent or poor, he is enclosed in a
role that society assigns to him without the ability to choose an
alternative or even to wage a resistance, either individual or
collective. A *psychological trap:* they are surrounded by a psychological culture that is widely diffused in the world of the
synopses. But that culture is perverted, its schemes are caricatural. Its interpretations have become mechanical, simplistic,
but above all completely deterministic. "Childhood trauma" is
a vulgarized descriptive tool used in sketches to explain the difficulties characters have in relationships, or their criminal profile: it is always integrated into the theme of the depossession
of self, but a cure is never envisioned. Quirks of the unconscious
determine compulsive behaviors that justify an irruption of arbitrary and sudden criminal acts that occur along a given line and
constitute the particular—and, it must be recognized, rather
effective—form of violence that is found in the synopses. Sex
is an essential dimension of relationships, but since relationships
are impossible, sex is experienced at the price of an instrumen-
talization of others. Repression is more serious than death. Guilt
more frightening than the sin. One can easily see how these
interpretations borrow from a psychoanalytic culture that permeates the world of the synopses just as it does the entire society. The media has contributed greatly to its diffusion: the work
of D. Cardon and S. Lascher on the radiophonic archives of
Ménie Grégoire[1] show that the sixties and seventies were the
years when the general public began to learn the elementary
notions of psychology, and that those notions gradually became

1. Ménie Grégoire was a radio personality who in the 1970s hosted a radio program that offered live psychological advice to listeners.

the common categories used to deal with relationships. And in being diffused, the notions became schematicized, became caricatural and lost their power to enlighten.

In a more general way, we find the same result for the way in which the social sciences are used throughout the material. The social sciences, at their inception, intended to be an agent for the amelioration of society by striving for a better understanding of its mechanisms. One wonders what happened, for them now to be found a century later in the corpus, diluted in the form of simplistic determinisms.

The knowledge of social givens, which is associated with the failure to envision any hope for liberation, leaves the characters in true disarray, prisoners in an iron cage, and convinced of the futility of action. The great systems of interpretation that were originally supported by a concern for understanding and the desire to effect change have ultimately turned against the objects of their scrutiny. They have provided arguments that support a culture of impotency.

All the great models of interpretation have mutually contaminated each other, to such an extent that now there is an unbearable tension: the strengthening of strategic representations of the individual is not very compatible with the notion that any repair of interpersonal bonds implies a free expression of the self. If the imperative of individual expression is not supported by a slightly positive social representation of interiority, if personal expression is necessarily a display of egotism and cynicism, it is highly unlikely that it will lead to an improvement of relationships (remember all the doors that slam and the couples who break up in the first lines of the synopses).

In fact, this situation points to a more general crisis, a crisis concerning the resources we possess to represent the world in which we live. Indeed, all the methods of interpretation we use to look at society were forged in the preceding decades. They were developed in a highly structured society. They are the heirs of the ideologies of liberation that saw the path to justice and freedom in the destruction of traditional social structures.

A contest of authority versus a structured order, union protest in a society of full employment, the liberation of women versus a patriarchal order, the desire for personal expression within a rigid order. But society has changed. Previous representations have lost their relevance. And for the time being there are no modern intellectual tools that might enable us to formulate things in a similar way. Any notion that stresses the limits of ideologies of liberation is automatically interpreted as a desire to cling to an old order. Since a return to the past is not in the picture, and the rise of individualism appears irreversible, and because no hope for regulation is apparent, there is impasse. From knowledge we slide to impotency. From impotency to pessimism.

THE SPIRAL OF PESSIMISM

The problem is therefore in part a problem of cultural resources, linked to the way in which we are likely to represent the world to ourselves. All the intellectual tools used by the authors to contemplate the current situation are instruments of criticism that have no normative supports: in contrast to a negative old order they propose a liberation that has not kept its promises, and are unable to produce alternative proposals. From the preceding decades the authors have retained a knowledge of the great determinisms, the recent evolutions, and the end of any hope for liberation.

This is not an unusual situation. Throughout history we have on many occasions witnessed the development of this inability of the available cognitive instruments to give shape to reality or to social needs. Ideas are disseminated, things change, but social representations preserve a certain inertia. Compared to the past, however, our age presents a unique characteristic that is connected to the existence of the mass media. Indeed, these media constitute a sound box that is unprecedented in history. The cultural contradictions that result from the gap between reality and the ideas we have to contemplate it are taken to an extreme degree, amplified and disseminated with a speed unequaled up to now. The effects of the autonomization of critical points of view and of their deviation into pure negativity are amplified and made extreme. This state of affairs might well explain the settling into a true *spiral of pessimism.*[2]

Yet it is not by looking at the positive elements of modernity through rose-colored glasses that one can halt the spiral of pessimism. The doubt concerning the cultural capabilities of our society is too deep not to render these voluntarist attempts at a restoration of optimism exasperating. Optimistic propositions are forever discredited: today they appear indecent (because they normally come from people who are protected), or perhaps manipulative (there is undoubtedly some money to be made by selling optimism, and ad agencies would be the first to grab it), or even quite simply idiotic. In reality, in order to alter the general climate of alarmism it is not enough simply to propose its reversal: any reparation must occur upstream. Hope is in the ability to understand how and under what conditions individualism might be an ideal.[3]

2. Using the expression "spiral of silence," Elisabeth Noëlle-Neumann described the process by which minority opinions are progressively excluded from the public stage. Here we have a crucial symmetrical and complementary phenomenon in which majority expressions are consolidated, support each other, and become extreme.

3. This expression is the title of Jean-Fabien Spitz's article in *Critique,* May 1993, where he presents the work by Charles Taylor, *The Ethics of Authenticity* (Cambridge, Mass., 1992).

The first phase of this work was carried out in collaboration with Dominique Pasquier and Dominique Jacquin. We divided the synopses up among us and analyzed them first by creating charts for each synopsis, including a summary of the authors' information and of the story, and a list of the themes involved. Each project was placed in a cardboard file folder on which a certain amount of information concerning the authors was noted (first name, last name, address, date and place of birth, previous experience). We worked separately for two months, and when we met again we realized the importance of the similarities we had noted: all our remarks were related; we had found the same things. Throughout this study the fact that our initial reading experience was so similar was of great help, for we were able to continue our discussions and monitor our proposed interpretations together.

The first step had enabled us to construct a systematic chart of the corpus following a preestablished pattern. The second stage could be more intuitive. I decided to focus on what had struck us so strongly while reading the texts—that is, a feeling of homogeneity—as a mystery. Where did it come from? Why did all these texts, apparently so different, seem to us to be so in tune with each other? What did they have in common?

To systematize our approach I ultimately[1] relied on the

---

1. Among our attempts to systematize the approach, a certain number of those attempts did not provide the results we had hoped for. Counting all the characters was a laborious undertaking, and a bit disappointing. Some were full of mean-

study carried out by Paul-André Rosental on the ties between microhistory and the work of Frédéric Barth.[2] My approach was as follows:

> To consider the corpus as a whole and present all the texts from the *arrangement* observed at the heart of the material. This meant not cutting the corpus up into pieces, like a fragmentary representation of disjointed objects, but proposing an "organization" that respected the general movement of the whole.

> To create categories upon which to base the analysis, starting with the texts themselves.

> To seek to reveal the principles that enable an understanding of those forms.

> To be sure that those principles enabled *all* the synopses to be taken into account, by granting the same analytical weight to them all. Texts that were obviously different from the others, those that stood out through their tone, their

---

ing. Others were transparent, purely conventional figures who weighed much too heavily in the columns. I then thought it necessary to grant more importance to the plots themselves, rather than to the characters and themes, and I again looked at the synopses to apply Greimas's *shéma actantiel*—Greimas's narratologic schema of "dramatis persona" that, following Propp, he describes as "Actants" (sender-receiver; subject-object; auxiliaries-opponents) (A. J. Greimas, *Du sens* [Paris, 1971]). See also Philippe Hamon, "Pour un statut sémiologique du personnage," *Littérature* 6 [May 1972]). But this was not very efficacious, either, as the synopses were too unfinished to lend themselves to a semiotic analysis; first, because in principle the synopsis is only a proposal for a screenplay that, itself, is only a film proposal. It is thus a prefiguration of a prefiguration. And a doubly amputated text cannot be the object of the same treatment as a completed work. By approaching it with a solemnity that it does not merit, it would be fixed in its intermediate situation, and undoubtedly any understanding of it would be destroyed. Then, the lack of rigor in the writing became truly problematic if one sought to adopt that perspective. There was a lack of negatives, certain paragraphs jumped around, characters were lost in midtext, they changed first names from one page to the next, unknown individuals arose from who knew where before vanishing just as mysteriously. In fact, the ability to master plot development is undoubtedly what most distinguishes amateurs from professionals.

2. Paul-André Rosental, "Construire le macro par le micro: Frédérik Barth et la *micro storia*," in *Jeux d'échelles: Micro-analyse et construction du social*, ed. Jacques Revel (Paris, 1996).

themes, and were statistically in the minority, were of as much interest, from the point of view of an understanding of the whole, as those that were in the majority.

To clarify all variants through the same processes: a single range of causal chains had to serve to understand the entire phenomenon in its heterogeneity.

I then set out again, starting not from the charts we had constructed, but from the entire collection of synopses, and I began to create new groups by assembling texts that resembled each other into piles, and then to look for the elements that created this resemblance. The files then began to circulate freely among the piles, and the synopses were classified and reclassified successively according to different criteria. This method, which presented a few disadvantages due to its unwieldy nature, did have the advantage of encouraging great familiarity with the material. Through this incessant work of classification and reclassification an understanding was developed. It was a matter of regrouping the texts by varying the criteria upon which the parallels were based. First, by following broad genres, then as a function of the subjects dealt with in the synopses, then as a function of the figures portrayed, which might be recurrent characters, or by the type of plots, the unfolding of events, the type of encounters, the modes of relationships, the forms of denouement, elements of context (scenery, atmosphere) or even the author's way of implicating himself in the synopsis, the information provided in the introductory material, etc. At each stage I put together texts that appeared to go together, not as a function of preestablished principles, but by keeping as close as possible to the synopses. The larger whole broke down into increasingly smaller segments connecting identical elements. From this I was able to reconstruct groupings that enabled me to develop organizing principles. Once these had been identified, I sought to take the exceptions into account. The synopses that remained "inexplicable" ended up in a pile that dwindled in the course of my work. This system, which led to regroupings based on heterogeneous principles of classification, had an advantage in that it revealed categories that we would not have imagined at the beginning of the study. We could then test the validity of the categories on secondary themes and characters. As the work went along, the initial divisions were broken up, split apart, and replaced by different ties, which were slightly overlapping, but more precise and more useful.

The next stage consisted of attempting to see how the material varied internally: I tried to find out if I could relate categories of authors and types of subjects. This approach provided a few preliminary results: the works of historical fiction were written by authors clearly older than the average (only six authors under thirty-five had chosen this genre). Among them were a certain number of teachers. Similarly, the authors who were born abroad, and particularly in North African countries, seemed particularly interested in the issue of immigration. In the category of outsiders, a very wide-ranging category, we found a few stories reflecting personal accounts, as well as— more often than in other categories—adaptations of works of fiction. I pursued my investigation, wondering whether the authors living outside Paris had the same sensibilities toward issues of social exclusion as Parisians did, whether those who lived in the suburbs or in the northeast part of Paris were more sensitized to the issues of the precariousness of living conditions than those in the south and west. I also wanted to know whether the male and female authors had the same way of viewing the evolution of relationships between men and women, whether they were easily placed within a particular genre, that is, sentimental comedies, detective stories, or science fiction. I thus continued to dissect the material, but each time I thought I had found something, I was forced to note the large number of counterexamples. *Obviously, the classic breakdowns were not very revealing:* there were no thematics that were truly specific to an identifiable group. No identifiable group was found solidly and exclusively in one subject category. (There was only one variable that was truly effective in dividing up the contents; this was the generational variable, the pivotal age being thirty-five, and only in that which concerned interpersonal bonds.) But I discovered something more: by proceeding in this way, that is, by seeking to divide up the material starting with the fragmentary data I had on the authors, I sensed we were losing what had seemed to us from the beginning to be the primary result of this research, namely, the incredible kinship that existed among these texts, the fact that all these synopses created a whole and seemed to be linked together.

However, before abandoning this approach, I told myself that the difficulties I was encountering were perhaps due to the fact that the information contained in the files was too sketchy. Therefore, in order to learn more, I decided to get in touch with the authors. In addition, I had to obtain their permission to publish the extracts of the synopses I wanted to use to illustrate my analysis. Following the letters I had written to three hundred of the authors, I received more than two hundred telephone calls that led to informal discussions, always very friendly and extremely interesting. I requested the authors' permission to ask three questions: I wanted to know how they had learned about the competition; whether they knew a lot about televised fiction; and whether they envisioned their writing activities as an entrée into a potential profession in the industry. But the most interesting part of the conversation was that which dealt with the screenplay project itself, the reasons for the choice of subject, the authors' intent. These exchanges were not part of the original research plan, and for deontological reasons I did not expect to use them in this work. Nevertheless, my reading and interpretation of the synopses was truly enhanced by these contacts: they changed my approach to the material because they corrected certain impressions that had, in fact, been linked to a lack of rigor in the writing. The way the screenplays were written had provoked a much gloomier view of the collection than I later had when I discovered meanings beyond words, since I had encountered the people behind the texts.

Following these conversations I carried out twenty-five in-depth interviews with certain authors whom I met in person. I had chosen them because they had significant profiles that enabled the clarification of the spotty data that appeared in most files. These interviews were an attempt to reveal any experience or training, and any strategies for penetrating into the milieu of audiovisual production. Our discussions dealt with screenplay writing, with training, the networks, the conditions of work in the profession, having a double profession, career prospects, as well as with the content of the authors' screenplay projects, their intentions in writing, the way in which they perceived the judges, and the way they envisioned their audience.

At the same time, the farther I went in this direction, one that was familiar to me (given the work D. Pasquier and I had undertaken previously on professionals in entertainment television), the more I had the feeling, not only that I was *not* clarifying the material, but that I was considerably restricting its significance. First, because I had a tendency to concentrate on the two categories of preprofessionals, that is, literati and practitioners in the realm of audiovisuals. But I was forgetting the outsiders. Now what was interesting in this screenplay competition was perhaps indeed that it had attracted people with quite heterogeneous profiles and that this heterogeneity did not have a recognizable impact on the themes chosen, at least not according to the information at my disposal. But I could not embark on the more extensive task of gathering the professional and biographical information on all the grandmothers, firemen, police inspectors, engineers, doctors, and professors who had responded to the call for screenplays. And above all, what would I have done with those biographies, how would I have interpreted them and connected them to the contents? However, if I did not take these outsiders into account (they did make up one-third of the sampling) and I concentrated only on the core of professionals and aspiring professionals in the field of audiovisuals, and then I analyzed the material as being significant of representations of a specific milieu, it was clear that I was obtaining an artificial result, since I had begun by eliminating from the group all those who didn't belong to it.

This was especially true as it was easy to see the temptation taking shape on the horizon as a result of this approach, a temptation to establish a summary parallel between the positions held by these aspiring authors and the contents they had devised: if the universe of the synopses was so gloomy, it was quite simply because it represented an imaginary of exclusion described by those excluded from the system. But I was not convinced of this interpretation. First, because the data in the files suggested I was dealing with rather unusual excluded types, since they represented a large, open spectrum of professions, from doctors to encyclopedia salesmen, including university professors and pizza vendors (even if the core group concentrated around the world of audiovisuals). Then, because from our telephone conversations I had learned that the people who had answered the call for screenplays were much more settled socially and professionally than I would have imagined from reading the synopses. Third, because actual films that had been shown, and which were by definition produced by people within the system, developed the same themes as those found throughout the corpus. Finally, because the position of being dominated in the realm of cultural production was not enough to account for the themes chosen, their unity and their coherence. For they could have just as easily been satisfied with promoting a rose-colored imaginary—one thinks, for example, of the writing of airport or train station novels. But above all, because I well understood that since I had been working with this material a number of references had become familiar to me, and because this work was constantly providing me with keys to an understanding of contemporary society that largely went beyond the limits of the corpus, even if I was not yet truly able to understand either how or why.

It was then that I understood that what gave the material its strength was not related to the *writers,* but to the *intended audience:* in fact, what made the corpus interesting was the fact that it was intended for television networks. It was defined by the address to which it was sent. It was clearly an error to see similar personal representations in it: we were in the realm of fiction, not in that of intimate journals or personal confessions. The authors did not necessarily believe in what they were writing, they were not necessarily connected to their texts. On the other hand, what was certain was that we were dealing with common anticipations. *It was because those hundreds of authors scattered over different sectors of society had assumed that a certain world had to be presented to some million or so viewers that this body of texts was so impressive.* It was not what the authors thought about the world or society in general that we had gathered: it was what they believed they should put in the public arena. Each one of them hoped to be chosen. Each author had therefore created a subject that he or she hoped would be the most appropriate possible from this perspective, and it was that sum of minianticipations that became crystallized in the corpus, by those numerous people who said to themselves: "If I do that, I'm sure it will work." Of course, those anticipations were not necessarily correct, since they did not always integrate the specific constraints of televised programming. There were obviously a number of possible psychological attitudes accompanying the challenge: some were cynical, others confident, some cautious, others provocative, disillusioned. There were also many different approaches, depending upon how accustomed the authors were to working in the medium, upon the degree of knowledge of TV programming, or of the rules of the TV game.[3] The range in the way intentions were structured

3. My conversations with the authors revealed an entire gamut of attitudes, which went from purely strategic approaches to those that would be considered purely disinterested. For example, some authors declared: "We took a completely 'marketing' approach. We told ourselves that on television you had to talk about social problems. And since racism is the primary social problem, we created a screenplay dealing with racism." Others, on the contrary, insisted that their approach was one of personal expression: "I really thought that if I spoke about that subject I wouldn't have a chance, but too bad. That was what I wanted to say." There was the entire gamut of intermediary positions. The biographical approach: "This story is the story of my life. I wanted to bear witness to it." A young woman, for example, had envisioned a script in which a young teacher from a working-class family from the North was confronted with a middle-class student. "That was my first plan, but I said to myself that if I made him a Polish miner's son, it wouldn't work, so I made him a second-generation immigrant." Another woman alluded to elements in her text that I didn't recognize. "Oh yes! that's right, you didn't have the version where he 'has' his girlfriend. I told myself that for prime time . . ." We can indeed see how the expectations of the producers were integrated into the projects. More or less well, moreover, for there remain many scenes in the material that could never be shown on television during prime time, many passages on difficult themes, such as drugs and incest, for example.

depended on the amount of knowledge each author had of the professional milieu, on his or her individual expertise, on the way in which they managed the tension between an artistic ideology that makes an artwork a place of personal expression, and the constraints that impose a submission to narrative rules, etc. But ultimately none of this was of any importance. In the end, what mattered was that they had all collectively assumed that those were the themes that were expected to be shown on television, that is, in the venue that is today the nucleus of cultural production and the center of the public arena.

From then on I was able to understand what this corpus had truly provided and why, from the beginning, it had fascinated me so greatly. I henceforth knew what my approach to it had to be. I was, of course, forced to acknowledge that the corpus was a little loose vis-à-vis the authors, and that, from that point of view, it raised more questions than it answered. But on the other hand, I had to anchor it as firmly as possible in the contents. All the same, if I examined the texts as a place where a development of social reality was taking place, and if I looked for the meaning of the corpus in the address where it was sent, the diversity in the origins of the texts did not constitute any limitation of the material's significance, but, on the contrary, it enriched the overall picture, for what mattered was less the point of departure than the place of arrival.

It was in the work of Michael Baxandall, notably *L'oeil du Quattroceno,* that I found the elements that helped me support this new approach. Baxandall's study focuses on how the painting of the Renaissance was received. The author shows how the audience of that time viewed the works of art it encountered while carrying specific cultural baggage and was equipped with categories of perception that were very different from our own. Baxandall attempts, therefore, using diverse external sources, to reconstruct some of the representational conventions that the painter brought to his painting: he looks at the sermons of popular preachers, studies gestures from dance manuals, suggested color codes, geometry manuals, etc. We then see how the painting of Piero della Francesca, expressing his interest in problems of measurement or proportion, gave Florentine merchants the opportunity to have fun with a competency in geometry or commercial mathematics that they usually restricted to their professions; how the religious sermons of the preachers inspired the paintings of Fra Angelico, or how the painting of Botticelli borrowed from dance. Baxandall thus proposes a way of viewing works of art that completely renews the way we might previously have looked at those paintings, but he also introduces us to cultural information about the society that produced them. This is not done through a simplistic theory of basic reflection, but rather through revealing how common cultural schemas, references, and conventions were at play, elements that the artist imported into his painting with the assumption that they would be understood by his contemporaries, and through which he contributed to a complementary enrichment of a common culture. Baxandall's book deals with how a work of art was received, but since he places the painting at the very heart of a network of circular interrelations between the painter, the commissioner, and the audience and establishes subtle ties between those four entities, it can just as easily be read inside out as a work on artistic production. This detour through Baxandall's work is obviously a bit surprising, but it does provide three essential ideas.

First, that these texts were the result of a *compromise* between what the author wanted to say as a form of personal expression, the way in which he integrated the expectations of the TV stations, and the way in which he anticipated the expectations of the audience. This compromise was achieved in various ways depending on the text and the author.

Next, that the authors had fed their texts with conventions placed at their disposal by *our common culture*. They had delved into a repertoire of schemas that belong to us all: these are references to movies, to advertising, to the universe of comic books, to popular literature. But also and above all they reflected a knowledge of society as it is transmitted through the media themselves, relying simultaneously on the rhetoric of televised news and that of documentaries and social programming. They had also utilized certain narrative processes of fictional writing, while counting on our abilities as ordinary viewers to interpret them, employing inversions, euphemisms, twisting, exaggerations, knowing that we would be able to replace, deflate, untwist, diffuse their words to discover meaning where they wanted to place it.[4] And thus we are able to derive the meaning and understand what the authors had intended to say. The authors did this every time, by relying on their idea of what we knew in common and of the way in which we would interpret it. And this play of *reciprocal anticipations* was what permitted us to reestablish the movement of common meaning.

The third, and clearly the most important idea, is that different cultural producers provide a complementary contribution to each other's work. (Baxandall writes: "Most of the time, paintings do not express their culture in a direct way, but rather in a complementary way. For it is as complements of culture that they are best able to satisfy the demands of the audience. The public hardly needs what it already knows.") That is, each work of art brings a specific contribution to the common edifice: diverse productions are influenced by each other, but they are not redundant. Each work proposes a particular version, starting from the

---

4. The conversations I had with the authors revealed, for example, the narrative procedures the authors intentionally used to give depth to their tales. They had recourse to processes of inversion ("if we showed elderly people as they truly are it would be too sad"), ("the elderly people we show are always so appropriate, I wanted to change things a little"); recourse to exaggeration ("Many men today are like that: pretty fragile and malleable. That's obviously an extreme case"); and recourse to euphemism: ("It's nothing compared to reality. In any case, it's so obvious that guys are more and more completely abandoned"). But in all cases the authors claimed to be starting with the intent to construct a form of reality, in the desire to describe social developments ("I wanted to sketch the character of a liberated modern girl who does what she wants, has no worries, has no reason for conscience. She doesn't reflect, she acts. I know a lot of girls like that"); to predict them ("I had written that before what happened in the suburbs, before that"); to predict them in order to prevent them ("It's up to science fiction to say: 'careful, we're going into the wall.'"); etc.

place from which it has come. This idea enables us better to understand the exact status of the material: indeed, it relies in part on the image of society that the media have given it (especially in the first two sections where we saw listed verbatim all the social problems as they are defined in the press, as if the authors had propped themselves on the rhetoric of newspaper stands,)[5] in part on the culture of a group, with generational rifts, and in part on individual aspirations influenced by the borrowing of post-Romantic artistic ideology. But it is the specific way in which these different sources are reworked, reshaped, and elaborated in order to elicit a meaning that makes them so interesting.

From those ideas it was possible to reconstruct an all-encompassing reasoning. Indeed, if I were right to grant more importance to what unified the texts than to what made them different, and to interpret them with regard to their content and not to their authors, and to consider that their audience was more important than the place from which they originated; if it is logical to arrange the texts following an axis that goes from the most exterior forms of social life through problematic forms of one's interpersonal life, to the most intimate forms of private life, and to consider that those three arenas hold together because they are presented at the heart of the same *continuum;* if it is justifiable to think that this material represents a particular point of view, situated socially, but one that has a general vocation, and that it is that dimension that matters at that moment, it becomes possible to put the corpus aside, to "ascend to generality," and to consider that these texts teach us something about society. But under the condition, all the same, that we be cautious, that we not slide into a theory of mere reflection, and that we start by looking at the specific character of these texts, with the fact that they are works of fiction organized around a crisis, and that we seek to identify that crisis.

5. Scanning the covers of four weeklies (*L'express, Le point, Le nouvel observateur,* and *L'evénement du Jeudi* during the six months that preceded the competition) confirmed this impression of conformity, except in that which concerned political issues and the international sphere.

Appendix 2:
The Authors

The announcement for the competition, "One Hundred First Works," was made through a communiqué transmitted to the press and to professional organizations. The people wishing to compete were to pick up packets that were available at the television stations' public-affairs offices in Paris, or in the provinces at the regional offices of France 3. Information concerning the procedure for entering the competition could be obtained on the Minitel. The jury, comprised of a certain number of audiovisual professionals as well as executives from the two stations,[1] were to consider the following selection criteria: "The degree to which a subject is treated in a new way, the age of the competitors, the feasibility of the project, and its ability to be accepted by the general public." Beyond that, the authors were completely free in their choice of subject.

The people who responded to the announcement were, by definition, people who hoped to become television screenwriters. In fact, they were more closely related to the world of image-makers than the organizers of the competition had anticipated. The data in their files enabled us to determine some of their characteristics. In-depth conversations allowed us to round out those characteristics.

1. The jury was comprised of Prune Berge, Marcel Bluwal, Fabrice Cazeneuve, Jean-Pierre Dusséaux, Maurice Failevic, Sylvie Fansten, Jacques Fansten, Alain Le Diberder, Patrick Lot, Serge Moati, Chantal Rémy, Claude Santelli, Josy Vercken, Françoise Verny, and Edith Vicaire. The quotation is taken from the text issued by the national television stations Antenne 2 and FR3, and signed by President Bourges announcing the competition, "One Hundred First Works."

The process used to select projects comprised several phases. The selection took place in four stages: out of the 1,200 projects received, 600 were eliminated after a first reading. Out of the remaining 600, 110 made it beyond a second reading. A third round of selection narrowed the group to 28 projects, and a final selection picked 12 that would then be edited further. The projects that were chosen, developed, and produced were aired in 1993 and 1994. The following description, based on the information contained in the authors' files, gives an overview of the authors' characteristics in relation to the selection process.

A Majority of Men

We must first note the following: the great majority of authors are men (71 percent as opposed to 29 percent women). A comparison with the gender ratio of comparable categories confirms the relatively weak participation of women in such situations: the active population includes 44 percent women, the category Professions in Arts and Entertainment Information indicates 50 percent women (Institut National des Statistiques et des Etudes Economiques [INSEE], job census 1989) and in the 1982 census, women represented 35 percent of the subcategory "literary authors, screenwriters, and dialogue writers."

Table A.1. Gender of Authors by Stage of Selection Process

	Men	Women
Total	71%	29%
First selection	74%	26%
Second selection	76%	24%
The 110	65%	35%
The 28	(20)	(8)
The 12	(9)	(3)

Age: Young Creators

On the whole, the call for projects achieved its goal: it attracted a huge majority of young authors. Six authors out of ten were under thirty-five. The premium on youth is particularly clear in the group of twenty-eight projects chosen (three-quarters under thirty-five, and out of the projects planned for production eleven authors out of thirteen under thirty-five).

Table A.2. Age of Authors by Stage of Selection Process

	Under 25	25–35	35–45	Over 45
Total	10%	49%	34%	7%
First selection	14%	47%	31%	8%
Second selection	7.5%	51.5%	37%	4%
The 110	6%	44%	38%	12%
The 12	(2)	(9)	(1)	

It should also be noted that there were few very young authors (under twenty-five) who responded (fewer than 10 percent), and above all very few who were selected (only six authors under twenty-five in the "110"). Those over forty-five were even fewer in number (7 percent), but they were comparatively more successful in the selection process (thirteen were over forty-five in the "110") than any other age category, even if at the end of the selection the twelve authors chosen were clearly younger than the population as a whole.

Geographical, Urban, and Cosmopolitan Origins

Geographical origins are analyzed here based on the author's place of birth, which does not enable us to distinguish nationalities clearly, since according to INSEE one-third of the people born outside France are considered French by birth (for example, repatriates from Algeria, or children born during their parents' stay abroad).

We can note two important facts: the preponderance of urban origins, and the high proportion of authors born abroad. Four out of ten authors were born in the Paris region, and most of the authors who were born elsewhere in France (40 percent of the total) were born in urban centers. These are obviously figures that are much higher than the national average, but which, however, correspond to all the polls concerning artistic and intellectual populations.

Place of Birth

The same is true of foreign origins (one author out of five was born abroad), but more important, their proportions increased quite sharply as the selection process was carried out: foreign origins are twice as numerous in the group of projects selected than in the group of those that were rejected, and there are five authors born abroad out of the twelve authors whose projects were accepted.[2]

Table A.3. Place of Birth of Authors

	Paris	Provinces	Abroad
Total	37%	42%	21%
First selection	42%	42%	16%
Second selection	36%	41%	22.6%
The 110	29%	43%	28%
The 28	32%	40%	28%
The 12	(2)	(5)	(5)

Place of Residence: Parisians

The first thing we notice is that eight out of ten authors live in the Paris region (as compared to one French person out of five). We are therefore in a schema of hypercentralization, a once again classic phenomenon within intellectual or artistic professions. The authors who are residents of Paris are concentrated in the northeast quarter of the capital (Ninth, Tenth, Eleventh, Eighteenth, Nineteenth, and Twentieth Arrondissements) as well as in the suburbs. The fact that neighborhoods in the west and in the Latin Quarter are not represented is not very surpris-

2. On this point we can refer to other studies that have been done concerning artistic and intellectual professions, all of which show a percentage of foreign origins from 20 percent to 25 percent, which increases with the notoriety of those under study.

ing, given the high prices of real estate in those areas. It must be noted, however, that the arrondissements in the south of Paris (Thirteenth, Fourteenth) are no better represented; these are arrondissements that had been occupied in large part by the intellectual middle-class at the end of the 1970s.

Table A.4. Place of Residence of Authors

	Paris Region	Provinces	Abroad
Total	81%	17%	2%
First Selection	82.4%	16.2%	1.2%
Second selection	78%	20%	2%
The 110	84%	11%	6%
The 28	(23)	(3)	(2)

The proportion of those living in the provinces drops sharply in the group of those selected; there are none in the final group of twelve authors chosen (who are all Parisians, except for two who live abroad).

Professional Profiles

In fact, if we look at the authors with respect to their professional associations, we are forced to note a wide range in the positions held: we span a broad spectrum of jobs going from white-collar professions to the world of irregular work. This said, such remarks are not very important in that the projects bring together people of different ages who are therefore at various stages in their professional lives, the youngest working primarily in the food industry. It is therefore not the authors' actual professions that is the point of comparison here. From the point of view of interest to us, it was better to compare them with regard to the activity that connected them within this framework, that is, that of screenwriting. And the data in their files enabled us to construct an index of professional integration, for the authors had indicated their previous experiences in their personal information. We could therefore distribute the writers along a radial going from the center to the periphery, some already being inscribed within audiovisual milieus, others having had experiences in training workshops, others, finally, who had no previous experience at all. We could therefore classify them by the way in which they defined themselves, beginning with the authors' degree of experience in the profession.

The profession of screenwriter is a hybrid one since it involves a work of writing that is placed in the service of the image. It therefore comes out of a double breeding ground, that of people who have writing ability and seek to branch out into the audiovisual, and that of people who carry on trades in the realm of the audiovisual and seek to write the text that will be used as a foundation for the film they wish to produce. Here we find the contrast that in France characterizes the situation of screenwriters, involved in the difficult autonomizing of their profession from the time, following the powerful blow of the New Wave directors, that the director succeeded in being recognized as the principal author of the work, thereby disqualifying his two other protagonists, the screenwriter and the producer.[3] We can therefore place our authors within three categories of approximately equivalent importance:

Literati.   Those whose talents are in writing. What enables them to be distinguished rather clearly is that they do not envision producing their projects themselves. They represent more than one-third of the population of screenwriters, which is a considerable number. But above all, they easily moved through the selection process: they represent one-third of the authors in the third selection and a quarter of those finally chosen.

Among them there are around fifty who acquired some initial experience in writing serialized fiction, generally in the realm of light fiction (*Plots, Misadventures, Passion, In the Event of Happiness, Neighbor, Neighbor*). Small in number at the beginning, they did, however, easily pass the first selections, and two of them ended up in the group of projects chosen.

Others have some experience in the theater, advertising, the press, or publishing. They hope to enter into audiovisual

---

3. Yann Darré, "Sociologie de l'art: Les créateurs dans la division du travail, le cas du cinéma d'auteurs," in *Sociologie de l'art,* ed. R. Moulin (Paris, 1986).

production to diversify their activities: a large number of them are playwrights and theater directors, journalists, writers or concept people in advertising, comic book writers, and of course writers, authors of short fiction or of novels (which they sometimes planned to adapt) either published or not.

Practitioners in the audiovisual.   This category includes directors in television or of institutional films and sometimes even of movies, as well as assistant directors. There are also those who work in technical professions in the visual media or advertising: scripters, film editors, photography directors, framers, photographers, graphic artists. There are many former film school students. But the majority of the group is made up of people who have already directed short films. They responded to the call for projects in great numbers, and the young authors-directors of short films are very well represented in the final selections.

Outsiders.   These represent one-third of the authors. They are those who have no professional experience in the realm of writing or of audiovisual production. This category comprises on the one hand young beginners and on the other people with composite professional profiles working in very diverse professions (post office employee, teacher, police inspector, Air France stewards, doctors, lawyers, architect, electronics expert, travel agent, accountant, chemist, agricultural expert, stone cutter, carpenter, etc.) We also note a strong presence of actors (there are more than one hundred who sent in projects). These *outsiders* responded to the call for projects in great numbers, but they had trouble getting through the selection process: none succeeded in reaching the final stages.

The in-depth conversations we held suggested ways of pursuing sociological studies of those who aspire to be an author. We saw clearly how the movie industry continued to focus all the hopes of the young. We saw the important role of schools such as FEMIS (Institut de formation et d'enseignement pour les métiers de l'image et du son—founded in 1986) both in training and the forming of professional networks, but also the importance of technical branches (the Louis-Lumière school), the specific role of departments in cinematographic studies, and even the communication departments of universities—which functioned more as indicators of the interest shown by the student in the realm than as a way to gain access to the milieu. We also saw how the two profiles we had distinguished—the literary profile and the audiovisual-practitioners profile—ended up in slightly different modes of professional involvement. Those who have a literary profile generally combine their writing initiatives with the practice of another profession, one that is often very unskilled for the youngest (menial jobs in the food industry), more skilled and therefore more engaging for older people. Sometimes the job also involves writing abilities, which is the case of journalists, in particular. Those who have a profile in telecommunications often hold technical jobs in that arena as their primary professions, and these jobs are held with the prospect of waiting, in the hope of then being able to go into directing. Participating as a technician in feature-length films is considered a way of entering into the production of a project and compensates for the disappointments of one's lower status as compared to one's hopes. This situation is all the more easily endured in that it is seen to be temporary.[4]

Finally and above all, our conversations revealed the essential role of the short film as a mode of professional socialization, with its completely characteristic type of organization: young beginners within the framework of a small production company that they themselves have sometimes founded find institutional financing (through the Centre national du cinéma, through regional funds, etc.) and succeed in carrying out their project by becoming connected within sympathetic networks and by collaborating with actors and audiovisual technicians who work for free or for a small fee—the participation of these professionals is explained in part by the fact that they thus acquire work expe-

4. See the work of Dominique Pasquier on television screenwriters, "Les mines de sel: Auteurs et scénaristes de télévision," *Sociologie du travail,* January 1994, and "Si Molière écrivait des *sitcoms,*" in *L'art de la recherche: Essais en l'honneur de Raymonde Moulin,* ed. Pierre Michel Menger and Jean Claude Passeron, La Documentation Française (1994).

rience that then enables them access to social rights.[5] Next, an entire process begins that starts with the renting of a room for a private viewing, to which friends, relatives, journalists, and if possible professionals from the milieus of televisual and cinematographic production are invited; then there is participation in the national and international festivals of short films, with the winning of prizes, if they are chosen—a process that culminates in the purchase of the film by a television station, and eventually its airing. Short films constitute a testing ground for a feature-film project, while at the same time the production company, in order to survive, diversifies its activities by making corporate or institutional videos.

These conversations thus enabled us to uncover a true professional milieu that is currently being constructed, a few indicators of which, moreover, enable us to see its amplitude and recent development.[6] The audiovisual sector exercises an obvious attraction on a growing proportion of young people who have been marked by a culture of the audiovisual, who see in a career oriented toward the image the possibility of exercising

5. This system is described very well by Dorine Bregman in "Nouveaux entrants dans l'industrie cinématographique: Le court métrage comme voie d'apprentissage," *Réseaux,* November–December 1997.

6. For the year 1987–88, 8,445 students were enrolled in training programs for "information, communication" in universities, and 1,795 students were enrolled in audiovisual training programs (degrees in telecommunications and film; technical degrees in telecommunications, Maîtrise en Sciences et Techniques and Magistère, third cycle); source SFSIC and Direction des enseignements supérieurs.

If one looks at the development of those in some of the professions in entertainment between the *censuses* of 1982 and 1990, we note a sharp increase: technical assistants in the production of shows have increased by 116 percent, going from 7,880 to 17,072; those in the artistic development of entertainment have increased by 40 percent, going from 4,020 to 5,644; technical producers of shows have increased by 120.5 percent, going from 4,180 to 9,216. According to the Emploi poll, jobs in telecommunications and in entertainment between 1983 and 1989 have gone from 34,927 to 48,624.

According to the data from the *caisse des congés-spectacles,* between 1968 and 1989, the number of executives and part-time technicians benefiting from the *caisse des congés-spectacles* has increased almost tenfold, going from 2,213 to 20,112.

I wish to thank Janine Rannou for giving me these partially unpublished data, which have come out of her research on the job itineraries of casual workers in telecommunications and entertainment.

a creative urge, and orient themselves toward the writing of screenplays all the more willingly in that that activity is accessible without demanding any particular training. At the same time the weight of the French tradition of the author/director continues to be felt.

Out of the 1,120 scenario projects that were sent to France Télévision, 12 were selected, edited, then produced. Some of them were aired in 1993, and others in 1994. Here is a list of the subjects of the projects. (These summaries are taken from the press releases sent out at the time the prizes were awarded.)

L'age de raison by Olivier Robinet de Plas

Agnès surreptitiously takes her brother Jérémy out of the psychiatric hospital where he was committed. But Johnny, another patient and friend of Jérémy's, joins them.

L'argent fait le bonheur by Robert Guédiguian and Jean-Louis Milési

A housing project in the poor neighborhoods of Marseille is afflicted with all the contemporary ills: delinquency, drugs, AIDS, racism. Exasperated parents, brought together by an extraordinary priest, will find an unusual remedy: in order to rediscover a warped solidarity, it is necessary to steal only from the rich.

Au feu les cahiers! by Patrick Chaize

In a school outside Paris a group of children rebel against the authoritarian teaching of a few adults who are somewhat overwhelmed by *zapping* and by the Ninja Turtles, and who are above all too inattentive to the true needs of the children. They rebel against the injustice aimed at one of their group who is threatened with expulsion for having been implicated wrongly in the misdeeds of some petty local gangsters. After two teachers are completely exhausted, a third is able to tame them.

Chemin de terre by Yves Elie

Surrounded by highways and supermarkets, Bernard, forty years old, refuses to sell his farm and his land to the Euro-Apéro trust. He lives alone and has only one friend, Schulz, a former legionnaire who runs a "fritobus" set up on the edge of his land. Maria, a Portuguese prostitute, little inclined toward compromise, comes with her mobile home to complete his neighborhood.

Grossesse nerveuse by Denis Rabaglia

The idea of becoming a father never occurred to Martin, the marketing director for a company selling meat for dogs, even though he detests the canine race. Thus when his girlfriend Ingrid tells him she is pregnant, he goes through the anguish of paternity.

La petite du placard à balais by Françoise Decaux-Thomelet

Paris, right before Christmas. The Bastille quarter, Aligre, Charonne.

Carla, twelve years old, and her mother who is fleeing her turbulent love affair with the angry Julien, move into the building where Raoul, ten years old, lives. One night, Carla's mother gets back together with her former and fearsome lover Julien, and Carla, furious with her, takes refuge in a broom closet connected to Raoul's bedroom.

La vie pratique by Christine Dory

Sylvie is twenty-five. She lives a life that is extremely close to the norm: she has embraced the social law as one enters a convent. The film tells how she breaks with this too-voluntary conformity by accepting a dirty deal, and how she will not recover from it.

Le poids du corps by Christine François

To please her father, a little girl who is both submissive and rebellious (Cécile) for years accepts the demanding discipline of artistic skating, but in the end refuses the yoke of the life of a champion. Having just become an adolescent, having just been touched by new desires, Cécile cannot get out of the trap of her father's love except by putting herself in a position to fail completely. Her failure (during the first Junior Championship of France competition) will be her most brilliant (and tragic) victory.

Twist Again by Moussa Sène Absa

The 1970s and pop fashion unfold over the youth of the working-class neighborhoods of Dakar. Here people are named Johnny Halliday, Sylvie Vartan, Mick Jagger, or Sheila. Identifying with these stars makes the adolescents live in a world of comic books and music, onto which each person projects his own story, dreams of his future. It is the leisure-time genius of adolescence that escapes parents, the final space of freedom before the awareness of adulthood. The silent movies they reinvent each evening accompany their dreams. Then one day, the first black-and-white television set appears in the neighborhoods.

Le rêve dans le coeur by Mitchell Hooper

1957. The Southwest. Henri and Suzanne are a couple of happy communists. The conjugal peace is broken by the arrival of an old friend of Henri's, Louis, who has come to work in Spain for the Front de Liberation National. Suzanne will help him, Henri refuses.

Les bois transparents by Pierre Sullice

Alex, a young painter who lacks inspiration, leaves Paris to live at an old sheep farm in the Cévennes. He has brought his girl-friend Véro with him. However, far from helping his work, the isolation of the Cévennes hills only contributes to the gradual destruction of the couple. Léo, a Down's patient who has es-caped from a home nearby, becomes the catalyst for this breakup, then the unwitting instigator of a new painting.

Revoir Balombé by Roland Cros

Boubacar, a young Senegalese immigrant, travels through France at the wheel of a forklift (the Fenwick type), which he drove for a company in the suburbs of Paris. From setbacks to good luck, his wandering leads him back to Africa, to his native village, where unexpected uses will be found for the machine.

Titles and Authors of the Synopses Cited

L'age de raison [The Age of Reason] by Olivier Robinet de Plas

L'amour en quatre [Love Times Four] by Marie Guilmineau

Les anachroniques [The Anachronics] by Christophe Jean Elie

L'ange-gardien [Guardian Angel] by Dominique Jeanjean

Après la vie, la vie, ou le cimetière des éléphants [After Life Is Life; or, The Cemetery of Elephants] by Frédéric Kocourek

L'argent fait le bonheur [Money Brings Happiness] by Robert Guédiguian and Jean-Louis Milési

Les arnaqueuses [The Lady Swindlers] by Laurent Gassiole

Au départ, c'est dur [In the Beginning It's Hard] by Jean Yves Lhoste

Au feu les cahiers! [Burn the Notebooks!] by Patrick Chaize

Au risque de s'y perdre [At the Risk of Being Lost in It] by Benjamin Rataud

A vot' bon coeur [To Yer Good Heart] by Irène Sohm

Bala ani Sôna [Bala ani Sôna] by Mohamed Camara

Bébé-cloche and *Parfum fatal* [Baby Bell and Fatal Perfume] by Bernard Ollivier

La belle vie [The Good Life] by Christophe Morin

La belle vie [The Good Life] by Bertrand Eluerd

Ben et Binette [Ben and Binette] by M'Baye Ousmane William

Les bois transparents [The Transparent Woods] by Pierre Sullice

La brèche [The Breach] by Dominique Sels

La brèche [The Breach] by Henri-Louis Poirier

Le bureau [The Office] by Jocelyne Thévenin

Le business d'Harmonie [Harmony's Business] by Marc-Henri Dufresne

Cado [Cado] by Jean-Louis and Roland Cros

Le canari bleu [The Blue Canary] by Lucie Ranson and William W. Wegimont

Caravane [Trailer] by Bernard George

Chemin de terre [Dirt Path] by Yves Elie

Le choix d'aimer [The Choice to Love] by Alexandra Marin

Clair obscur [Murky Light] by Noël Dupont

Comme des fantômes [Like Ghosts] by Jacques Maillot and Yves Bernanos

Contre-courant [Countercurrent] by Michel Granvale

Les déchaînés [The Wild Ones] by Francis Parisot

Le départ [The Departure] by Luc Leblond

Dernier round [Final Round] by France Vachet

Les deux soleils [Two Suns] by Lucie Ranson and William W. Wegimont

Les douaniers [The Customs Officers] by Bernard Jeanjean

Double exposition [Double Exhibition] by Marie Arnaud

Doutes d'hiver [Winter Doubts] by Jacques Brac de la Perrière

Embrasse-moi [Kiss Me] by Paul Gueu

L'entracte [Intermission] by Jacques Bertrand

L'entrave [The Shackle] by Jean Pierre Marivot

Entremise [Intervention] by François Barluet

L'envol [The Flight] by Pascal Coinchelin

L'espoir manqué: L'espoir qu'un jour! [Vanished Hope: The Hope That One Day!] by Philippe Guignard

Et pourtant la Seine coule [And the Seine Flows On] by Philippe Boeffard

Le feu sacré [The Sacred Fire] by Catherine Burucoa

Le flux et le refus [Flow and Refusal] by Bernard Perrin

Fortuné [Fortunate] by Guy Lafages

La Fugue [The Runaway] by Pascal Laethier

Un fusil et des bonbons [A Gun and Some Candy] by Benjamin Rataud

Futur ordinaire [Ordinary Future] by Pierre André Sauvageot

Grossesse nerveuse [Nervous Pregnancy] by Denis Rabaglia

Histoire d'Amour [The Story of Love] by Frédéric Ville

Histoire ordinaire [Ordinary Story] by Daniel Cotard

L'homme sans frontière [The Man without Borders] by Jean-Claude Jean

Ils s'appelaient Atlantide [They Called Themselves Atlantis] by Philippe Zenatti

L'important, c'est d'y croire et quand on n'y croit plus, de faire semblant d'y croire [What's Important Is Believing, and When You Don't Believe Anymore, to Pretend to Believe] by Pascal Delaunay

Irma la naze [Irma the Fool] by Catherine Benguigui

J'ai sorti mon chien du congélateur [I Took My Dog Out of the Freezer] by Bernard Jeanjean

Jonas ou le tableau dans la jungle [Jonas, or the Painting in the Jungle] by Claude Soret

Les journées perdues d'une famille ordinaire [The Wasted Days of an Ordinary Family] by Dino Gambini

Laurent et les sixties [Laurent and the Sixties] by Hervé Larroque

La légende de l'homme de boue [The Legend of the Man of Mud] by Alain Lefèvre

Léon [Leon] by Vincent Baur

La lézarde [The Crack] by Bertrand Schmitt and Michel Leclerc

Lili [Lili] by Pascal Roigneau

Les lubies de Lola [Lola's Whims] by Gerry Meaudre

La manchette [Headlines] by Gilbert Libé

Martin a du style [Martin Has Style] by Pierre Zeni

La mésange et le hérisson [The Titmouse and the Hedgehog] by Jean-Luc Rougny

Les mutins de l'Arche [The Mutineers of the Ark] by Bertrand Schmitt and Bernard Leclerc

Naissez, nous ferons le reste [Be Born, We'll Take Care of the Rest] by Patrice Duvic

Norbert, présentateur-télé [Norbert, TV Announcer] by Paul Chamussy

Nous étions trois [There Were Three of Us] by Hafid Nour

Onc' Damien [Unc' Damien] by André Mineux

Le palais des merveilles [The Palace of Wonders] by Cécile Cabel

Papillons en folie [Butterflies Out of Control] by Karine Douplitzky

Les papys flingueurs [The Killer Grandpas] by Frédéric Karpyta

Paris/Saint-Pétersbourg [Paris/St. Petersburg] by Henryk J. Mrozowski

Paroles de fleurs [Flowery Words] by Dilip Sandiressegarane

Pas de mouron dans les mouroirs [No Worries in the Death Houses] by Dominique Jeanjean

Pauvre Martin [Poor Martin] by Michelle Robert-Reich

Pesé, compté, divisé [Weighed, Counted, Divided] by Brigitte Aubert

La petite du placard à balais [The Little Broom Closet Girl] by Françoise Decaux-Thomelet

Les petites annonces [Classified Ads] by Laurent Louis

Une petite ville bien tranquille [A Small, Very Peaceful Town] by Marie Arnaud

Le poids du corps [Body Weight] by Christine François

Le portrait [The Portrait] by Bernard Rapatout

Pour la dernière fois, Jérôme Vasselin a perdu la tête [For the Last Time, Jérôme Vasselin Has Lost His Head] by Suzanne Sanchez

La preuve par sang [The Proof Is in the Blood] by Catherine Tullat

Professeur Rousseau [Professor Rousseau] by Marc Blouet

Protz et Schmutz tv [Protz and Schmutz TV] by Philippe Muller

Pygmalionnes [Ms. Pygmalions] by Christine Koechlin-Jancovici

Qu'est-ce qu'on fait des restes? [What Do We Do with the Leftovers?] by Christophe Delmas and Luc Gentil

La queue [The Line] by Jean Leclerc

Rap Side Story by Pascal Mauconduit

Ratonnade [Arab Bashing] by Laurent Bouhnik

Le retour des palombes [The Return of the Doves] by Mamady Sidibé and Françoise Simon

Le retour d'Hélène Kramp [The Return of Hélène Kramp] by Catherine Hertault and Jean-Luc Seigle

Le rêve dans le coeur [A Dream in Your Heart] by Mitchell Hooper

Les rêves en miettes [Dreams in Crumbs] by Eric Bitoun

Revoir Balombé [To See Balombé Again] by Roland Cros

Les Rhododendrons [The Rhododendrons] by Robert Hemard and Jean Maurice Ooghe

Roberto, Roberto, mon amour, ou le portefeuille imitation écaille [Roberto, Roberto, My Love; or, The Imitation Tortoiseshell Wallet] by Annie Fitoussi

Le rouge et le vert [The Red and the Green] by Sophie Garnier

Le royaume du Siam [The Kingdom of Siam] by Jean Maffioletti

Sale temps pour les pigeons [Lousy Weather for Pigeons] by Pierre Barachant

Secteur d'enfer [Sector of Hell] by Pierre Bordage

Si c'était lui, ce ne sera pas moi [If It Was He, It Won't be Me] by Michèle Dalbin

La sirène des Pyrénées [The Mermaid of the Pyrenees] by Marc Eisenchteter

Sortie blanche; secteur d'enfer [Exit Blanche; Sector of Hell] by Pierre Bordage

Les spirales de l'inquiétude [Spirals of Concern] by Roland Stevenot and David Anemian

Syn pour la vie [Synthesized for Life] by Armand Wahnoun and Jean Pierre Lazar

Taupe secret ["Top Secret"] by Evelyne Houdeyer

Les terrains vagues [Vacant Lots] by Nicole Jaouen

Thérèse et les transports en commun [Thérèse and Public Transportation] by Marie Annick Le Guern

Une trajectoire de papillon [Trajectory of a Butterfly] Dynn Aedela

Twist Again by Moussa Sène Absa

La vie en HLM [Life in the Projects] by Liliane de Merindol

La vie petite [The Little Life] by Sylvie Simon

La vie pratique [Practical Life] by Christine Dory

Vous n'en reviendrez pas! [You Won't Get Over It!] by Caroline de Knyff and Vincent Louky

Voyage à l'ombre [Voyage into the Shadows] by Jean Pierre Marivot

Bibliography

Alberoni, Francesco. *L'amitié.* Paris, 1985.

———. *Le choc amoureux: L'amour à l'état naissant.* Paris, 1985.

Allen, Robert. *Speaking of Soap Operas.* Chapel Hill, N.C., 1985.

Badinter, Elisabeth. *L'un est l'autre.* Paris, 1986. Translated by Barbara Wright as *The UnOpposite Sex: The End of the Gender Battle* (New York, 1989).

Barth, Frédérik. *Process and Form in Social Life.* London, 1980.

Barthes, Roland. "Introduction à l'analyse structurale du récit." *Communications* 8, 1969.

———. *S/Z.* Paris, 1970. Translated by Richard Miller as *S/Z* (New York, 1974).

Baxandall, Michael. *L'oeil du Quattrocento.* Paris, 1985.

Becker, Howard S. *Art Worlds.* Berkeley, 1982.

———. *Outsiders: Studies in the Sociology of Deviance.* New York, 1963.

Boltanski, Luc. *La souffrance à distance.* Paris, 1993.

Bourdieu, Pierre. *La misère du monde.* Paris, 1993.

———. "La production de la croyance: Contribution à une économie des biens symboliques." *Actes de la recherche en sciences sociales* 13 (Feb. 1977).

———. "Projet créateur et champ intellectuel." *Les temps modernes,* no. 246.

Bregman, Dorine. "Nouveaux entrants dans l'industrie cinémato-graphique: Le court métrage comme voie d'apprentissage." *Réseaux,* November–December 1997.

Caillois, Roger. *Anthologie du fantastique.* Paris, 1966.

Cassata, Mary, and Thomas Skill. *Life on Daytime Television: Tuning-in American Serial Drama.* Norwood, N.J., 1980.

Chalvon-Demersay, Sabine, and Dominique Pasquier. *Drôles de stars: La télévision des animateurs.* Paris, 1990.

———. "Le langage des variétés." *Terrain* 15 (1990).

———. "La naissance d'un feuilleton français." *Réseaux,* special issue, 1991.

Chambat, Pierre, and Alain Ehrenberg. "Les *reality shows:* Nouvel âge télévisuel?" *Esprit* 1 (1993).

Chamboredon, Jean-Claude. "Marché de la littérature et stratégies intellectuelles dans le champ littéraire." *Actes de la recherche en sciences sociales* 4 (July 1975).

Champagne, Patrick. *Faire l'opinion: Le nouveau jeu politique.* Paris, 1990.

Chauvenet, Antoinette, G. Benguigui, and Françoise Orlic. "Le personnel de surveillance des prisons: Essai de sociologie du travail." Report to the Minister of Justice, 1992.

Cottereau, Alain. "L'invention d'un espace public démocratique et l'expérience du réél social." Communication aux journées d'étude du CEMS, 8–10 December 1993.

Darnton, Richard. *The Great Cat Massacre and Other Episodes in French Cultural History.* New York, 1984.

Darré, Yann. "Sociologie de l'art: Les créateurs dans la division du travail, le cas du cinéma d'auteurs." In *Sociologie de l'art,* ed. R. Moulin. Paris, 1986.

Dayan, Daniel. "A la recherche du public." *Hermès,* 11–12 April 1993.

———. "Les mystères de la réception." *Le débat* 71 (1992).

Dayan, Daniel, and Elihu Katz. *Media Events: The Live Broadcasting of History.* Cambridge, Mass., 1992.

Douglas, Mary. "La connaissance de soi." *Revue du Mauss* 8 (1990).

Dubet, François. *La galère: Jeunes en survie.* Paris, 1987.

Duhamel, Olivier, and Jérôme Jaffré. *L'état de l'opinion.* Paris, 1991.

———. *L'état de l'opinion.* Paris, 1992.

Dupont, Florence. *Homère et Dallas.* Paris, 1990.

Eco, Umberto. "James Bond: Une combinatoire narrative." *Communications* 8 (1969).

Ehrenberg, Alain. *Le culte de la performance.* Paris, 1991.

Escarpit, Robert. *Le littéraire et le social: Eléments pour une sociologie de la littérature.* Paris, 1970.

Geertz, Clifford. "Form and Variation in Balinese Village Structure." *American Anthropologist* 61 (1959): 991–1012.

Goffman, Erving. *The Presentation of Self in Everyday Life*. Garden City, N.Y., 1959.

———. *Stigma: Notes on the Management of Spoiled Identity*. Englewood Cliffs, N.J., 1963.

Greenberg, Bradley S. *Life on Television: Content Analyses of U.S. TV Drama*. Norwood, N.J., 1984.

Greimas, A. J. *Du sens*. Paris, 1971. Translated by Paul J. Perron and Frank H. Collins as *On Meaning: Selected Writings in Semiotic Theory* (Minneapolis, 1987).

Hamon, Philippe. "Pour un statut sémiologique du personnage." *Littérature* 6 (May 1972).

Heinich, Nathalie. "L'art et la profession: Les traducteurs littéraires." *Revue française de sociologie* 2 (1984).

Hennion, Antoine. "L'industrie de l'art: Leçons sur la médiation." *Réseaux*, July–August 1993.

Katz, Elihu, and Tamar Liebes. "Six interprétations de la série *Dallas*." *Hermès*, 11–12 April 1993.

Kaufmann, Jean-Claude. *La chaleur du foyer: Analyse du repli domestique*. Meridiens, 1988.

Lasch, Christopher. *The Culture of Narcissism: American Life in an Age of Diminishing Expectations*. New York, 1978.

Léridon, Henri, and Catherine Villeneuve Gokalp, with Laurent Toulmon. *Constance et inconstances de la famille: Biographies familiales des couples et des enfants*. Travaux et documents, no. 134, PUF-INED, 1994.

Lévi, Giovanni. *Le pouvoir au village*. Paris, 1989.

Lipovetsky, Gilles. *Le crépuscule du devoir: L'éthique indolore des nouveaux temps démocratiques*. Paris, 1992.

———. *L'ère du vide: Essais sur l'individualisme contemporain*. Paris, 1984.

Matelski, Marilyn. *The Soap Opera Evolution*. Jefferson, N.C., 1988.

Mehl, Dominique. *La fenêtre et le miroir*. Paris, 1992.

———. "La télévision compassionnelle." *Réseaux*, January 1994.

Menger, Pierre-Michel. "Rationalité et incertitude de la vie d'artiste." *L'annéiologique* 39 (1989).

Morin, Violette. *L'écriture de presse*. Paris, 1969.

Moulin, Raymonde. *L'artiste, l'institution, le marché*. Paris, 1992.

Noëlle-Neumann, Elisabeth. "The Spiral of Silence." *Journal of Communication* 24 (1974).

Pasquier, Dominique, with Sabine Chalvon-Demersay. "Les mines de sel: Auteurs et scénaristes de télévision." *Sociologie du travail* 4 (1993).

―――. "Si Molière écrivait des *sitcoms.*" In *L'art de la recherche: Essais en l'honneur de Raymonde Moulin,* ed. Pierre Michel Menger and Jean Claude Passeron. La Documentation Française, 1994.

Pharabod, Anne-Sophie. "Perdu de vue: Ethnographie d'un *reality show.*" M.A. thesis, Paris X–Nanterre, 1993.

Puiseux, Hélène, ed. *Cinéma: Rites et mythes contemporains. EPHE* 1–15.

Quéré, Louis. *Des miroirs équivoques.* Paris, 1982.

Radway, Janice A. *Reading the Romance: Women, Patriarchy, and Popular Literature.* Chapel Hill, N.C., 1982.

Raimbault, Ginette. "Morceaux de corps en transit." *Terrain* 18 (1992).

Rannou, Janine. *Les métiers de l'image et du son.* Ministère de l'éducation nationale, CEREQ, Paris, 1992.

Renaut, Alain. *L'ère de l'individu.* Paris, 1989.

Ricoeur, Paul. *Temps et récit.* Paris, 1983. Translated by Kathleen McLaughlin and David Pellauer as *Time and Narrative* (Chicago, 1984).

Rosental, Paul André. "Construire le macro par le micro: Frédérik Barth et la *micro storia.*" *Jeux d'échelles: La micro-analyse à l'expérience,* ed. Jacques Revel. Paris, 1996.

Roussel, Louis. *La famille incertaine.* Paris, 1992.

Sels, Dominique. *Eden en friche.* Paris, 1990.

Sennett, Richard. *Authority.* New York, 1980.

―――. *The Fall of Public Man.* New York, 1976.

Simon, Jean-Paul. "Médiations et histoire sociale de l'art." *Réseaux,* July–August 1993.

Spitz, Jean-Fabien. "L'individualism peut-il être un idéal?" *Critique,* May 1993.

Sullerot, Evelyne, Simone Berton, and Claude Bremond. "Les héros des films dits de la Nouvelle Vague." *Communication* 1 (1961).

Taylor, Charles. *The Ethics of Authenticity.* Cambridge, Mass., 1992.

Terrier, Michel. *Individu et société dans le roman américain de 1900 à 1940.* Paris, 1973.

Théry, Irène. *Le démariage.* Paris, 1993.

Thiesse, Anne-Marie. *Le roman du quotidien.* Paris, 1984.

Wieviorka, Michel. *La France raciste.* Paris, 1992.

Index

Absa, Moussa Sène: *Twist Again*, 175

Action Thématique Programmée, CNRS Continuous Observation of Social and Cultural Change, 136n. 2

actors, representation of, 81–82, 121

adolescence, number of screenplays about, 29

Aedela, Dynn: *Une trajectoire de papillon*, 42

Africans, immigration and, 57, 59–63

age, of authors, 95, 118, 154, 164–65. *See also* adolescence; children; elderly; youth

Age de raison, L' (Robinet de Plas), 173

Agoult, Marie d', 9

Alberoni, Francesco, 122

alcohol, in psychological dramas, 24

Ame a du bon, L', 13

Amour en quatre, L' (Guilmineau), 120

Anachroniques, Les (Elie), 117

Anemian, David: *Spirales de l'inquiétude, Les,* 53

Ange-gardien, L' (Jeanjean), 109

Angelico, Fra, 160

animals, protection of, 39

answering machines, implications of, 17

Antenne 2 (station), 163n. 1

anticipation: rational, 137; reciprocal, 161

Après la vie, la vie, ou le cimetière des éléphants (Kocourek), 68

Argent fait le bonheur, L' (Guédiguian and Milési), 42, 173

Arnaqueuses, Les (Gassiole), 39

Arnaud, Marie: *Double Exposition*, 97; *Petite ville bien tranquille, Une,* 102–3

art: handicapped people associated with, 75–79; number of screenplays about, 29; as profession, 26, 89; reception of, 159–62; redemption through, 18, 79–82; religion associated with, 79; as work, 81–83, 89

artists: aesthetic values and, 79–82; foreign origins of, 166n. 2; representational conventions of, 159–62; as symbolic, 36, 89

Aubert, Brigitte: *Pesé, compté, divisé,* 38

audience, influence of, 157–59

audiovisual practitioners, authors as, 169, 170–72

1; crisis for, 31–34, 139–40; description of, 119; duration of action and, 18–19; as fragmented subjects, 132–37, 140–41; gender of, 23; generational context of, 94–97, 140; geographic location of, 19–23; historical context of, 8–18; homogeneity of, 35; main vs. secondary, 28, 30, 35; meanings of, 27, 64n. 5; money's impact on, 87–89; positive vs. negative, 89; powerlessness of, 145–48; religion of, 30; social worlds of, 23–27, 31–32, 87–90; as victims, 56; as wanderers, 130–32. *See also* artists; doctors; elderly; handicapped people; heroes; immigrants; policemen; real estate developers

Chasseur français, Le (magazine), 112

Chemin de terre (Elie), 22, 174

childhood, as marvelous, 68n. 6

childhood trauma, 146

children: decision to have, 98–100; divorce's impact on, 101n. 4; elderly as, 68–69; number of screenplays about, 29; parental relations with, 95–96; parents sought by, 100–101; sexuality and, 96–97; social bonds of, 70–71; as symbolic, 68; as victims, 71–72

Choix d'aimer, Le (Marin), 106

Clair obscur (Dupont), 42, 96, 98

Coinchelin, Pascal: *Envol, L'*, 76–77

collective action, mobilization of, 48–49

comedy: drama compared to, 4; elderly in, 63–64, 69–70; geographic location in, 20; journal-

ists in, 85; pregnancy in, 99; real estate developer in, 48–49

Comme des fantômes (Maillot and Bernanos), 77–78

communitarianism, concept of, 142

computer science, knowledge of, 70

Contre-courant (Granvale), 44

Cotard, Daniel: *Histoire ordinaire, L'*, 87

countryside. *See* rural areas

Cour des miracles, Une, use of term, 75n. 7

Courteline, Georges, 45

crime, types of, 38–42. *See also* police dramas; violence

crimes of passion, 30, 112. *See also* police dramas; violence

crisis: components of, 35–37, 142–45; identification of, 6, 31–33, 139–45, 147–48; of institutions, 32–33, 34, 90; in interpersonal bonds, 140–41, 147; music's role in, 83; of paternity, 101n. 4; pessimism about, 144–45; policemen's role in, 37–47; power in, 90; real estate developers' role in, 47–52; in social bonds, 32–33, 34, 90, 140–41. *See also* interpersonal bonds; social bonds; solitudes

Cros, Jean-Louis: *Cado*, 99

Cros, Roland: *Cado*, 99; *Revoir Balombé*, 59, 176

customs officials, representation of, 42

Dalbin, Michèle: *Si c'etait lui, ce ne sera pas moi*, 99

Dallas (U.S. television series), 94

death, in screenplays, 24

Naissez, nous ferons le reste (Duvic), 12

newspapers: as evidence of context, 162n. 5; as invaders, 84. *See also* journalists; media

Noëlle-Neumann, Elisabeth, 149n. 2

Norbert, présentateur-télé (Chamussy), 86

Nour, Hafid: *Nous étions trois,* 59–60

Nous étions trois (Nour), 59–60

Ollivier, Bernard: *Bébé-cloche,* 42, 70

Onc' Damien (Mineux), 105

Ooghe, Jean Maurice: *Rhododendrons, Les,* 48–49

ordinary lives, emphasis on, 9

organ transplant specialists, representation of, 52, 54

outsiders, authors as, 169

Palais des merveilles, Le (Cabel), 80–81

Papillons en folie (Douplitzky), 106–7

Papys flingueurs, Les (Karpyta), 66, 69

parents: children's search for, 100–101; representation of, 95–96; sexuality of, 96–97

Paris, authors' place of residence in, 166–67

Parisot, Francis: *Déchaînés, Les,* 15–16, 87

Paris/Saint-Pétersbourg (Mrozowski), 20

Paroles de fleurs (Sandiresse-garane), 51–52, 70

Pas de mouron dans les mouroirs (Jeanjean), 67

Pasquier, Dominique, 2, 151, 156

Paul et Virginie, 114

Pauvre Martin (Robert-Reich), 78–79

Perrin, Bernard: *Flux et le refus, Le,* 45–46

Pesé, compté, divisé (Aubert), 38

pessimism: prevalence of, 34, 144–47; spiral of, 148–49

Petite du placard à balais, La (Decaux-Thomelet), 174

Petites annonces, Les (Louis), 111–12

Petite ville bien tranquille, Une (Arnaud), 102–3

Piero della Francesca, 159–60

plastic surgeons, 52, 54

plots: evaluation of, 151–52n. 1; summaries of, 173–76; thematic elements in, 4–5, 27–31, 154–55, 157, 159

Poids du corps, Le (François), 30, 175

Poiré, Jean Marie, *Visiteurs du soir, Les,* 115, 117n. 6

Poirier, Henri-Louis: *Brèche, La,* 98–99

police dramas: death in, 24; number of, 29; themes in, 132; time in, 39; types of crime in, 39–42. *See also* policemen

policemen: gangs and, 62–63; models of, 36–37; powerlessness of, 37–47

polio, representation of, 78

Portrait, Le (Rapatout), 117

Pour la dernière fois, Jérôme Vasselin a perdu la tête (Sanchez), 54

power: in interpersonal bonds, 104–8; of media, 83–84; of professions, 89–90

powerlessness: of characters, 145–48; of institutions, 37–47, 90, 139–40; of journalists, 83–84; of policemen, 37–47

Preuve par sang, La (Tullat), 97

priests, representation of, 42, 79

prison workers, representation of, 42